eat
feel
fresh

eat feel fresh

Sahara Rose Ketabi

Contents

Foreword

We are living in a time where the masses are waking up to the connection between the mind, body, and spirit. This connection is not new, but rather an age-old wisdom stemming from Ayurvedic tradition in ancient India over 5,000 years ago. We are observing that our bodies are synchronistic displays of our spirits; that our physical health is a reflection of our internal state of being; that the way we eat impacts the way that we feel.

Ayurveda is a subject I have deeply studied and wrote about in this lifetime. My book, *Perfect Health*, published in 1991, was the first to popularize Ayurveda in the West and bridge it with modern medical science. I have dedicated my entire career to adapting ancient Vedic teachings to today's times so they can be experienced by today's people. And I stand proud that millennials like Sahara are continuing to share and modernize this wisdom, so it can live on for future generations in our ever-changing global climate.

Ayurveda is a living science; one that has transformed and moved throughout the centuries to match the needs of the individuals it serves. Yet its tenets remain the same: the foods we eat become the very foundation of our bodies, seeds of our thoughts, and essence of our consciousness. Everything that we consume contains an energetic effect, and through food, we change the entire fabric of our being.

More than ever, we must bridge the worlds between science and spirit, ancient and modern, Eastern and Western. Sahara's theory on "Alkaline Ayurveda" displayed in *Eat Feel Fresh* deeply reflects the importance of consuming a nutrient-dense, plant-based diet that incorporates the physical, mental, and spiritual bodies, all of which are deeply connected. The very illusion of separation is what has held us back from health in the past.

In Vedanta there is an expression, "As is the atom, so is the universe; as is the microcosm, so is the macrocosm; as is the human body, so is the cosmic body." This is the very essence of what Sahara shares in *Eat Feel Fresh*. We are deeply attuned to nature, which provides us with the instincts we need to maintain balance. Ayurveda helps us uncover and sharpen these instincts, so we can make better choices for our overall well-being.

I highly recommend this book to anyone who feels called to take a deeper look at the foods they eat and the implications it has on their mind, body, and soul. Sahara Rose is a millennial thought-leader who is taking the torch of Ayurveda and burning it brightly. This is the second book of hers I have had the pleasure to introduce and an example of her dedication to modernizing Ayurveda so its wisdom can transcend time. Let it inspire you to make food choices that serve not only your body, but also your spirit.

—Deepak Chopra, MD

Introduction

What if I told you that I could tell a lot about your personality just from hearing about your digestion? If you were anything like I was six years ago, you'd have a hard time believing it.

AN AYURVEDIC AWAKENING

Flashback to 2012: I'm sitting in the humble waiting room of an Ayurvedic doctor waiting to be seen. Pictures of Hindu deities adorn the wall—Durga riding a tiger, Saraswati sitting atop a lotus, and Dhanvantari, the four-armed God of Ayurveda. I see a monkey playfully dangling out the window, looking for his next meal; a familiar sight in New Delhi. I don't have cell phone service, so my eyes drift to a poster of a meditating woman with colorful circles stacking up the centerline of her body; muladhara chakra, svadisthana chakra, manipura chakra. This office is a far cry from the hyper-sanitary doctors' offices in Boston where I had spent a huge part of the past year trying to figure out what was wrong with me, but at this point I'm willing to try anything to unravel the mysteries of my health.

I'm given a client intake form and start filling out the questions. "How is your digestion?" "How is your sleep?" The questions are off to a predictable start, but they soon become a bit more personal. "What sort of dreams do you have? Are you floating, fleeing, or flying? Are they realistic and problem-solving? Are they romantic and sweet?" I wasn't sure why I was being asked about my dreams in a digestion consultation, but hey, it's India, you never know what you'll be asked, so I go with the flow.

A jubilant woman in a red sari approaches me with a welcoming Namaste and a deep bow.

"My name is Dr. Priyanka Gupta, I'll be seeing you today. Please follow me."

I follow her through the office, the pungent scent of oils and herbs dancing in the air. This earthy smell is a stark contrast to the whiffs of Febreeze and hand sanitizer that usually accompany my visits to a medical establishment. I sit on the chair and stare at her three-foot-long braid, wishing my own could grow that long and lustrous. She reviews my health and personality assessment, and to my surprise, just about begins telling me my life story.

"Oh, a LOT of Vata, I see. You must have trouble sleeping. Staying up at night thinking. You think too much."

Okay, maybe she noticed the bags under my eyes, I think.

"Your joints always cracking. Crack, crack, crack. You're too young to have back pain."

Can she see that my posture is off? I wonder as I sit up straighter.

She proceeds to look at my tongue and take my pulse.

"Very low *agni*," she tells me, which I later learn means "digestive fire."

"Agni very low, not digesting food properly. Body not taking in the nutrients. Though you are eating, body is malnourished."

Malnourished? I am literally eating all day, I think, envisioning the suitcase of snacks I brought with me on my three-month volunteer trip to India.

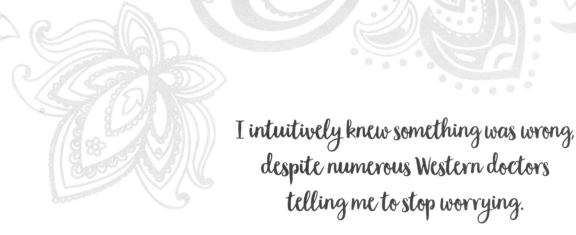

I intuitively knew something was wrong, despite numerous Western doctors telling me to stop worrying.

"Agni so low that body shutting down. No more period. Very, very bad. You are too young for this."

Okay, I told her all about my digestion and dreams, but how does she know about my period?

It was true. My period had been MIA for over a year now. At first I didn't pay too much attention to my period's absence—what girl wants her period? But after a year without it, I intuitively knew something was wrong, despite numerous Western doctors telling me to stop worrying and just get back on the pill.

"No period very serious. You have all Vata (air energy) imbalances: cold body temperature, dry skin, bloating, gas, constipation, no period, weak muscles, cracking joints, insomnia, anxiety, worrying too much. If you continue like this, later in life you can get osteoporosis, Alzheimer's, and worst of all, no baby. You too pretty to not have baby."

Wait, wait, wait, hold up. Did I just hear the words osteoporosis, Alzheimer's, and infertility? This can't be possible. I'm a Holistic Health Coach and pretty much a raw vegan. My life is *dedicated* to health. I have my own raw-vegan nutrition blog, Eat Feel Fresh, and eat all the kale in the world. There is no way this can be accurate.

"There has to be a misunderstanding," I tell the doctor. "I eat a really healthy diet—big leafy green salads, green smoothies with spirulina, açai bowls, flax crackers…" I continue listing the things I eat on a daily basis in the US.

"Acha, this is why you have so much Vata. No more cold, raw, dry foods. Only cooked foods. Mung *dhal* (mung beans) and white basmati rice with lots of ghee."

"Yeah, see the thing is I'm mostly raw-vegan so I can't eat any of those foods. Can I just take some herbs instead?"

"No beta, this is Ayurveda way."

Well, this isn't going to work out, I think as I leave the office with a list of "dos" and "don'ts" in my hand. All my favorite foods are on the "don'ts" and all the heavy foods I stopped eating years ago to lose weight are on the "dos." I figure that if I were to ever follow an Ayurvedic diet, I'd gain 50 pounds along the way and backslide to my overweight years as a young teenager. I had spent the past few years trying to lose weight and wasn't going to risk gaining it back.

SEARCHING FOR ANSWERS

I went on my way, trying to self-heal with the power of Google. That year was a blur of dietary experimentation. I went paleo, keto, macrobiotic, low FODMAP, gluten-free, grain-free, and everything in between. I had flings with the Candida diet, SIBO diet, GAPS diet, and every other acronym you can imagine. I went to every kind of doctor and did every type of blood test under the sun (somehow managing not to faint). Yet I still couldn't find the answer to my issues. I was told by a gastroenterologist that I had IBS, or irritable bowel syndrome (the blanket term for, "you have digestive issues that we can't figure out"), and was told by an endocrinologist that I had hypothalamic amenorrhea (this loosely translates to, "you aren't getting your period and we're not sure why... seems like it's all in your head"). They told me it really wasn't that big of a deal that my body was essentially shutting down and prescribed me IBS medication and birth control to mask the symptoms. *Oh, don't worry, honey. There's a pill for that.*

I didn't want a quick-fix or a Band-Aid solution. I wanted to get down to the root cause of the problem. Why wasn't my body functioning properly despite my healthy diet and young age, at only 21 years old? Finally, as a last resort I came back to Ayurveda, the ancient Indian health system focused on digestion.

I acknowledged that I had a severe Vata imbalance in my system, which essentially made my body cold and dry from within. My digestive "fire" had become so weak that I wasn't breaking down foods, assimilating their nutrients, or discarding their waste, hence the perpetual bloating. The excess air in my system was materializing as gas and my dehydrated colon was causing constipation. Although I thought I felt fine, my mind and body were in a constant state of stress, which I perceived as normal. I was always on the go, working late into the night and squeezing intense workouts into my demanding schedule, thinking I was super committed to fit in a cardio kick-box session on an already busy day. Isn't that dedication?

Well, as it turns out, the Vata air energy within me had turned into a tornado, tossing all of my bodily systems into chaos. Everything from my menstrual cycle to circadian rhythms, which are all based on digestion, felt the turbulent effects. What I needed most was not another juice cleanse or spin class, but to slow down and build heat, reconnecting to my grounding Kapha (earth) energy and increasing my transformative Pitta (fire) energy.

It all made sense to me on an intuitive level. My quest for the "perfect" body and the "perfect" diet had made me totally out of touch with my body and wreaked havoc on my digestion. I was listening to doctors and following other people's advice rather than listening to my own experiences. I had heard of the mind-body connection, of course, but never connected the dots in my own life. I hadn't realized that the excess air in my body had created excess air in my mind, or that the constant bloating and continuous feeling of cold were directly related to anxiety and insomnia. I was astonished and eager to learn everything about this relationship. I decided to go back to India and sign up for Ayurveda school.

CREATING AN ALKALINE VERSION

I loved the wisdom of the Ayurvedic diet for its intuitive and customizable nature, but longed to create a way for it to be more alkaline, plant-based, and low-glycemic. During my studies in Ayurvedic nutrition and cooking and in apprenticeships in South India, I was continuously developing ways to adapt the recipes for a modern, alkaline kitchen. I used my Vata imaginative energy and got creative, crafting recipes following Ayurvedic guidelines with a refreshing plant-based approach. Instead of wheat-based bread, I'd use vitamin-rich almond flour. In place of rice, I'd use protein-packed quinoa. Instead of ghee, I'd use nourishing plant-based sesame oil. As a substitute to cane sugar, I'd flavor with sugar-free pure monk fruit sweetener. In lieu of dairy milk, I'd pour hormone-balancing flax milk. Instead of heavy cream, I'd use skin-loving coconut. Rather than cheese, I'd use nutritional yeast or make my own nut-based versions. Instead of heavily cooking my food, I'd lightly sauté it to preserve its nutritional benefits. Little did I know, I was creating the foundation for what would later become this cookbook.

During my studies, I also realized how much the food industry has changed in the past 5,000 years. Dairy and wheat, two staples of the traditional Ayurvedic diet, have been particularly affected by genetic modification and pesticide use. Many people today, myself included, grew up consuming extremely acidic, processed foods that simply weren't around in ancient India. As a result, we are experiencing a rise in gut issues such as candida and SIBO (small intestinal bacteria overgrowth), as well as a multitude of physical and mental disorders that are directly linked to our food industry. In fact, an estimated 80 to 90 percent of Americans have an acidic pH. Scientists have found that cancer can only thrive in an acidic environment, and that the body handles excess acidity by producing fat cells to absorb the acid and neutralize it. Therefore, consuming an alkaline diet is the best way to naturally find your body's healthy weight and to ward off diseases.

Alkaline foods are also lighter on the body. Whereas 5,000 years ago, people worked as farmers and led extremely active lifestyles, today we have become much more sedentary, spending most of our days behind a computer. We no longer require the energy provided by large amounts of carbohydrates and instead need more alkalizing vegetables to enhance our energy levels, cleanse our systems, and uplift our spirits.

Alkaline foods also combat toxins in the environment. From the moment we are born, we are exposed to environmental, household, personal-care, and pharmaceutical toxins. In ancient Ayurvedic times, the *rishis* wrote about these pollutants, called *garvisha*, which causes *ama*, toxins, in the *dhatus*, tissues. However, they could not have predicted how polluted this world has become, nor could they have predicted how many wrong turns the food industry has taken. Living in today's world, we need to include even more alkaline, organic, plant-based foods in our diet to flush away the toxins we're exposed to on a daily basis.

Shortly after adapting these changes in my diet, I felt better—not just in my body, but also in my mind. My digestion, menstruation, and sleep became regular, harmonized with the sun and moon. The constant state of restlessness I carried—needing to always be doing something and going somewhere—was replaced by a deep sense of inner-peace and acceptance, similar to the tranquility one feels at the end of a yoga class. I realized that Ayurveda is so much more than a way to heal the body—it actually shifts the very foundation of your being. Brillat-Savarin once said, "Tell me what you eat and I'll tell you what you are," but I say, "Tell me how you digest, and I'll tell you who you are."

DISCOVERING MY DHARMA

They say you don't choose your path, but your path chooses you. My path was to remain in India for two years studying Ayurveda, continuously reading, absorbing, and translating these texts into a modern language that my blog readers could understand. I intensely studied every book about Ayurveda, starting with *Perfect Health* by Dr. Deepak Chopra, and later the many works of Dr. Vasant Lad, Dr. Kshirsagar, Dr. Douillard, and Dr. Frawley. Eventually, I wrote *Idiot's Guides: Ayurveda*, sharing my modern approach to Ayurvedic wisdom with many American households and inspiring a new generation of Ayurvedic practitioners.

Learning about Ayurveda was like relearning a language my soul had spoken for a thousand lifetimes. The theories intuitively made sense to me, and oddly enough, whenever I had a question while writing my books, I tuned in and realized that somehow I already knew the answer. I truly believe this isn't my first life teaching Ayurveda, and part of my *dharma*, life purpose, is to modernize this ancient healing science so it can become accessible to more people, the way its sister science, yoga, has become over the past decade.

Ayurveda is not a diet, but rather a system that offers a deeper introspection on food and life. Ayurveda is a living science, one that has adapted across the centuries to fit the needs of the people it serves. It went from being the leading medical system in India to an underground kitchen science during British rule, and it is only now beginning to resurface. This flexibility is what has made Ayurveda the world's oldest health system that is still practiced today. I believe the time has come for Ayurveda to spread its wings and open its doors so people across the world can benefit from its age-old wisdom (without having to move to India, though recommended).

The holistic view of Ayurveda is more vital now than ever before. So many people, like myself, have grown tired of jumping from diet to diet, looking for the answer to health when it already exists inside of us. All it takes is tuning in and listening.

Ayurveda provides us with the language to explain what our bodies already know. As you read this book, you too may experience a remembrance of wisdom passed down through your ancestral lineage, no matter where in the world your roots are from. The tenants of Ayurveda are echoed across the globe: that the solution to health is to live in harmony with our nature. We are ready for a return to a system of eating that encompasses and nourishes our bodies, minds, and spirits, all of which are interconnected in ways we never could have imagined.

Ayurveda provides us with the language to explain what our bodies already know.

WELCOME TO EAT FEEL FRESH

Eat Feel Fresh is the renaissance of Ayurveda: a refreshed, plant-based approach to Ayurvedic cuisine, which I call Alkaline Ayurveda. It celebrates the healing vibration that plants offer and marries ancient wisdom with globally-inspired, plant-based, alkaline recipes. It honors the sacred tradition of Ayurveda, while incorporating ingredients that weren't available in ancient India, like chia seeds, avocado, and tahini. It remixes your favorite dishes, like tacos, pizza, brownies, and lattes, while sneaking in healing Ayurvedic herbs and spices, like turmeric, ginger, and ashwagandha to nourish you along the way. It shows you that Ayurveda is not limited to only traditional Indian foods—you can follow Ayurvedic guidelines and include plant-based ingredients from around the world. *Eat Feel Fresh* is an Ayurvedic playground, where spices and ingredients take on new forms and presentations but remain grounded in the same ancient tradition.

Eat Feel Fresh invites you to look at food in a whole new way. Rather than focusing on calories, you focus on qualities. Rather than focusing on macronutrients, you focus on tastes. Brilliantly enough, the two actually reflect one another. I'll show you how the effects of food go far beyond the nutritional label, so you never have to look outside of yourself for food choices again.

Just as there is no one-size-fits-all approach to health, there also isn't one for your diet. I'll teach you how to customize your recipes for your unique mind-body type, your *Dosha*, so you can make the right food choices for what you need, when you need it. Not only will these recipes address physical imbalances, but also common mental ones we may experience on a daily basis: anxiety and insomnia, which are related to excess Vata; impatience and irritability, which are related to excess Pitta; and loneliness and depression, which are related to excess Kapha. These emotions are simply messages from our bodies that it's time to tune in and pay deeper attention within. I'll also demonstrate ways you can adjust the recipe for your Doshic needs so you don't have to make individual dishes for everyone in your family. (In fact, it's unheard of in India for each person to receive their own custom meal, even in the homes of Ayurvedic doctors.) All it takes is a little tweaking to make a beautiful, tridoshic meal that works for all.

FOOD AS A PATH TO LIFE

This book is truly a love letter to the people of India who invited me into their homes and kitchens to cook with them. I came to India with the vision to shoot photography for this book, but instead of making a plan, I let the universe guide my course. Serendipitously, I was invited into the homes of countless incredible families to share a meal. We sat on the floor, laughing as we flipped rotis over a fire, made hot chai to serve the village, and picked fresh Ayurvedic herbs from the trees. Food truly brings community together and creates a mutual language of taste and nourishment. My experience in India has made me see how sharing a meal truly is the fabric of society and has made me rethink the many dinners I ate working over my laptop.

My hope is that *Eat Feel Fresh* will make you fall in love with cooking again. Food is divine medicine that is meant to be enjoyed—before, during, and after preparation. We begin the process of digestion the moment we put our hands on that special ingredient, and through active loving participation in the cooking process, we can increase the nutritional value of food. I offer you affirmations and mantras throughout the book to connect you with your meal on a deeper, more spiritual level.

Above all, this book is meant to show you that the foods we eat have a direct impact to the way that we feel. We take on the energy of everything that we consume and become happier, more aligned individuals by making the right food choices. We don't only digest food, but also thoughts and emotions. A healthy digestive system can gracefully catch the curveballs life throws at you and transform them into art. We carry the vibration of the foods we eat and the thoughts that we think, and this book will help you bring them both back into alignment. Our personalities are an expression of our meals and we can enhance our inner-peace, mood, mental clarity, and pleasure by nourishing our bodies on a cellular level.

Eat Feel Fresh is much more than a cookbook; it is a stepping stone to fulfilling your *dharma,* your purpose, on this beautiful planet. To heal the planet, you must first heal yourself. Health is not the end-goal, but rather the means to becoming your highest self. By evolving into the healthiest, most radiant version of you, you have more energy and joy to share with the world. Taking care of your well-being is the first brave step toward reclaiming your freedom and serving your mission on this planet. True health doesn't end with the self, but rather transcends out into the universe, creating ripples of healing across the planet.

I invite you to join me on this culinary journey across India. I'll meet you at the crossroads of ancient and modern, Eastern and Western, science and spirit, cultural and contemporary. *Namaskar.*

AYURVEDIC PRACTITIONER + AUTHOR

What Is Ayurveda?

Ayurveda, pronounced *aye-your-vay-duh,* is the world's oldest health system, originating in ancient India over 5,000 years ago. It's the sister science of yoga, focused on balancing the mind and body for radiant health.

MIND-BODY INTEGRATION

Ayurveda originates from two Sanskrit words: *ayur,* meaning "life," and *veda,* meaning "knowledge." In order to achieve balance, you must have complete knowledge of your entire life. Ayurveda is based on two guiding principles: 1) The mind and the body are inextricably connected, and 2) Nothing has more power than the mind to heal and transform the body.

It's important to note that "mind" is not synonymous with "brain." The mind is the manifestation of all mental states, such as thoughts, emotions, perceptions, beliefs, memory, and imagination. The brain is the hardware that allows us to experience these mental states. According to the *Vedas*—the ancient, sacred texts from which yoga and Ayurveda are both derived—the mind is defined as "the awareness of consciousness." The mind not only exists in the brain, but also in all parts of your body. Various *chakras,* regions in our bodies, have their own central intelligence, such as the heart and stomach.

Western medicine treats each part of the body and mind separately. There are gastroenterologists for our digestion, therapists for our minds, and endocrinologists for our hormones. An Ayurvedic practitioner will ask about all of these things, because there is no separation between them. In Ayurveda, all areas of health, from physical to emotional, are interconnected and treated in harmony. Ayurveda draws connections between bloating and anxiety, heartburn and anger, weight gain and depression, and offers ways to bring each issue back into balance.

DIGESTION IS KEY

In Ayurveda, it's not, "you are what you eat," but rather, "you are what you digest." Digestion is the cornerstone of all health, and if your digestion isn't strong, the rest of your body will fall out of balance. We digest not only food, but also pollutants, skincare and household products, and even thoughts and emotions—thus, we need a strong digestive system to break down, assimilate, and detox all that we take in. Digestion is what turns food into nutrients, thoughts into action, toxins into waste, and emotions into self-awareness. It's the ignition within us, and when it's weak, everything else goes haywire, from our skin to our hormones to our mood.

INTUITIVE, INDIVIDUAL TREATMENT

The cornerstone of Ayurveda is bioindividuality. We are each unique individuals with a combination of the three *Doshas,* or mind-body types: *Vata, Pitta,* and *Kapha.* There is no one-size-fits-all approach, because we each have highly individualized needs based on our unique Doshic constitutions. On top of that, our needs change on an annual, seasonal, and even daily basis, as the cyclical rhythms of the earth affect the biorhythms of our bodies, making self-knowledge extremely vital to our physical and emotional well-being. Overall, Ayurveda draws parallels where Western medicine sees incongruent lines. It sees the body as a complex machine that is a reflection of your state of mind.

Comparing Yoga & Ayurveda

YOGA	AYURVEDA
Based on *sadhana*, inner spiritual practice	Based on *chikitsa*, therapy or treatment
Comprised of meditative breathing and physical practice, as well as lifestyle and service	Comprised of nutrition, healing, and self-care practices, as well as meditation
Immediate goal is spiritual awakening	Immediate goal is mind-body balance
Ultimate goal is achieving *samadhi*, inner peace	Ultimate goal is achieving *samadhi*, inner peace

AYURVEDA AND YOGA

If you practice yoga, Ayurveda should definitely be part of your lifestyle, as the two are interconnected sister sciences that were meant to always be practiced hand-in-hand. In addition to a physical practice, yoga is also a spiritual practice with the goal of releasing attachment to your ego so you can become one with the universe. Perhaps you've had moments in your yoga or meditation practice when you felt so much greater than just your physical body and at complete oneness with all things—that was true yoga.

Ayurveda is the predecessor of yoga, more rooted in the mind and body. The ancient *rishis*, sages, who wrote the Vedas knew that one has to first have a pure, functioning vessel before they can go beyond it. Think about it—when you're sick, all you can think about is getting better. You aren't thinking about how to become your highest self—you are stuck in your physical body.

The rishis knew that the body's physical state could affect one's ability to transcend the ego. When your digestion is out of balance, or you're highly anxious, or you've broken out in hives, you are too distracted to become one with the universe. Therefore, you first must balance the mind and body with Ayurveda so you can truly practice yoga.

Though yoga and Ayurveda have different immediate goals, their overall purpose is the same: reaching *samadhi*, the ultimate state of inner peace. Samadhi is when you aren't affected by outside conditions, such as what other people around you say, how your body feels, or your own limiting beliefs. You are completely present in the moment and in tune with your highest self.

A Modern Approach to Ayurveda

Eat Feel Fresh is designed to embrace the most beneficial and salient aspects of Ayurveda, while letting go of other recommendations that were more relevant in ancient India than they are today. The greatest lesson you can learn from Ayurveda is to listen to your intuition and see that your body is a reflection of your nature.

TRADITIONAL AYURVEDA | EAT FEEL FRESH

Based heavily on grains— rice is the staple of each meal.

Based on a more alkaline, plant-based diet—vegetables, not grains, are the staple of each meal. The food industry has drastically changed since ancient times due to hybridization, pesticides, and fertilizers, which affect the nutrition of grain crops and animal products. As a result, many people experience digestive, hormonal, and autoimmune issues. An alkaline diet—a low-acid diet that limits or omits meat, cheese, eggs, and grains—helps bring the body back into balance. *Eat Feel Fresh* offers an alkaline, plant-based approach, and focuses on including more healthy fats in the diet, rather than carbs. You don't have to be totally plant-based, but vegetables should be the majority of your diet.

Relies on foods that were available in ancient India, where Ayurveda originated.

Uses modern, global ingredients that satisfy Ayurvedic guidelines. Ayurveda is not a diet, but rather a system of health and food philosophy. *Eat Feel Fresh* uses Ayurvedic ingredients, such as turmeric, cumin, ginger, and cardamom in a modern way. It also incorporates ingredients from the world's "Blue Zones," geographic regions boasting populations with the longest lifespans. These include sweet potatoes and avocados, as well as other superfoods, such as chia seeds. These ingredients may not have been available in ancient India, but they are beneficial for our health and shouldn't be avoided just to eat "Ayurvedically."

Doesn't allow raw foods, because the soil in India contains bacteria and parasites, which can make raw food dangerous for consumption. India is also an extremely hot country, so raw foods spoil quickly in the heat. Refrigerators didn't exist 5,000 years ago, so well-cooked foods were safer to consume.

Recognizes that raw foods are safe to eat and have been consumed safely for thousands of years. The important thing is whether you can digest raw foods. Those with more Pitta in their bodies can include more raw foods in their diets (though not a purely raw diet), while Vatas should include mostly cooked foods with a little bit of raw foods. Kaphas can have a combination. Most recipes in *Eat Feel Fresh* are cooked, but you are still free to incorporate raw fruits and vegetables in your diet for the living enzymes and vitamin C they contain, as long as you can digest them. Your body will tell you whether it likes raw foods or not—listen.

Doesn't allow fermented foods, because the heat in India does not allow for safe fermentation.

Believes that fermented foods are beneficial for your gut bacteria and have been consumed safely for thousands of years. Coconut yogurt, sauerkraut, and kimchi are wonderful sources of probiotics, which are especially important in a culture where bacteria-killing antibiotics are over-prescribed, and where our soil has been stripped of beneficial bacteria.

Forbids mushrooms, because many mushrooms in India are poisonous or psychedelic.

Accepts and loves mushrooms for their medicinal benefits—as long as they are safe to consume (stick to the ones in the grocery store).

Is rich in dairy, especially ghee (clarified butter) and paneer (cottage cheese).

Is dairy-free, because the dairy we have today is very different from that in ancient India, where cows were sacred and all dairy was raw and organic. Cows today are injected with growth hormones and antibiotics, which are transferred to their milk. On top of that, all dairy is pasteurized, making it void of the enzymes that make it digestible. Many people are unknowingly lactose-intolerant, and whether you immediately feel digestive issues or not, dairy causes mucus buildup in the system, which can facilitate illness. You can easily replace ghee with plant-based oils, and replace paneer with nut-based cheeses for a delicious alternative.

An Alkaline Upgrade

All foods are either acid-forming or alkalizing. In the past century, our diet has become increasingly focused on acid-forming foods such as meat, sugar, wheat, grains, and dairy, many of which are highly processed. To rebalance our pH levels and prevent disease, we must include more alkalizing foods in our diets.

ISSUES WITH ACID

When our bodies are acidic, our entire systems fall out of balance, causing weight gain, digestive issues, skin problems, fatigue, inflammation, a weakened immune system, muscle weakness, urinary tract issues, receding gums, and kidney stones, among other issues. An acidic body is the perfect environment for disease to spread. Viruses, bacteria, fungi, candida, and even cancer cells all thrive in an acidic environment. In addition to following Ayurvedic guidelines, the recipes in this book are also designed to create an alkaline environment in your body to prevent toxins from spreading in your system.

ALKALIZING AYURVEDA

The Ayurvedic diet traditionally includes more foods that are acid-forming or neutral, such as grains, dairy, and legumes, and fewer foods that are alkalizing, such as leafy greens, sprouts, and fresh herbs. Although this was a sensible and healthy way to eat 5,000 years ago, it's not an optimal way for us to eat today.

When Ayurveda was developed, all food was wild, organic, local, and seasonal. It was grown in fertile, mineral-dense soil, free of pesticides and fertilizers. Today, almost everything you find at the supermarket, even organic food, is hybridized, making it void of the proper mineral balance that wild foods contain. Many supermarket foods are also genetically modified, which results in a loss in nutrients and exposes the body to fertilizers and chemical pesticides.

Research from the University of Texas published in the *Journal of the American College of Nutrition* found that one would have to eat eight oranges today to get the same amount of vitamin A our grandparents would have gotten from just one orange. Between 1951 and 2002, potatoes lost all of their vitamin A, as well as 57 percent of their vitamin C and iron, while broccoli lost 63 percent of its calcium and 34 percent of its iron.

WHAT TO EAT

All of this means we need to consume more vegetables than ever before to get the nutrients we need. *Eat Feel Fresh* is about deriving the bulk of your calories from alkalizing plant sources, so you can balance your pH and reap as many nutrients as possible.

However, just because something isn't totally alkaline doesn't mean you should avoid it. We need some acid-forming and neutral foods for proper digestion, but should favor healthier types like whole grains, fermented foods, and legumes. Aim for about 80 percent alkalizing foods and 20 percent acid-forming foods, and limit or avoid the most acid-forming foods such as dairy, refined sugar, flour, and conventionally raised meat.

Note that a food's acidity does not correlate with its acidity in the body. For example, lemon and apple cider vinegar are acidic; however, the end products they produce after digestion and assimilation are alkaline. Therefore, they're alkalizing to the body.

Eat Feel Fresh Alkaline Chart

MOST ALKALIZING (ORGANIC ONLY)

leafy greens (spinach, kale, rainbow chard, arugula) • healing spices (turmeric, cumin, coriander, fennel seeds) • fresh herbs (cilantro, parsley, basil, mint) • sprouts and grasses (alfalfa, bean, pea, wheatgrass) • cruciferous vegetables (broccoli, brussels sprouts, cabbage, cauliflower) • non-starchy vegetables (cucumber, asparagus) • citrus • vinegar • sea vegetables (kelp, wakame, kombu) • algae (chlorella, spirulina)

MODERATELY ALKALIZING

avocado • coconut • starchy vegetables (sweet potato, carrot, beets, squash) • lettuce • zucchini • nightshades (eggplant, tomato, pepper) • pungent spices (garlic, ginger, onion) • quinoa • seeds (chia, hemp, flax) • monk fruit

MILDLY ALKALIZING

mung beans • adzuki beans • white beans • lentils • cold-pressed organic oils (avocado, coconut, sesame, flax) • raw nuts (almonds, walnuts) • nut and seed butters (almond, sesame, sunflower, tahini) • organic, non-GMO tempeh and tofu • organic, local, seasonal fruit

NEUTRAL

black beans • kidney beans • navy beans • chickpeas • buckwheat • brown rice • other nuts and seeds • stevia • pure birch xylitol

MILDLY ACID-FORMING

grains (basmati white rice, barley, oats, millet, amaranth, farro) • pickled vegetables • ghee • goat's milk dairy products • potatoes • most fruit (apples, bananas, berries, cherries, dates, papaya, plums) • low-mercury wild-caught fish • coconut sugar • raw honey • yacon syrup

MODERATELY ACID-FORMING

yogurt • eggs • coffee • miso • kombucha • kefir • cashews • peanuts • chicken • turkey • lamb • table salt • processed honey • maple syrup

MOST ACID-FORMING

GMO soy products (soy beans, soy sauce, soy protein) • alcohol • sugar (soda, desserts, agave) • flour (white bread, pastries, bagels) • cow's milk dairy products • red meat • shrimp • MSG • pesticides • artificial sweeteners

Ayurveda and Raw Food

Many people think that they cannot eat raw foods while following Ayurvedic guidelines, but that couldn't be further from the truth. Ayurveda is a living science—it adapts to the place, time, and needs of the individual—and that includes modern eaters who crave raw veggies.

DIFFERENT TIMES, DIFFERENT NEEDS

During the agricultural revolution, grains became more readily available and provided workers with sustained energy for physical labor. However, we are now in a different age—the Information age. Instead of working in factories or on farms, we spend our days sitting in front of the computer. We don't require as much physical energy as our ancestors needed centuries ago, but instead do better with more leafy greens, which are less calorie-dense and help to rid the body of toxins.

CONSIDER YOUR UNIQUE CIRCUMSTANCES

I came to Ayurveda after being a raw vegan, and at first the cooked foods felt so great on my digestive system. However, after two years of eating almost all cooked foods, I started to crave salads and smoothies again. I thought, "What's wrong with me? This isn't the *Ayurvedic* way!" I felt guilty about wanting raw foods, the same way one would about doughnuts. As I became more self-aware, I realized that I was putting myself in another box, from strict raw vegan to strict "Ayurvedic." I wasn't embracing the *true* message of Ayurveda: that it is meant to adapt to your unique needs. I was living in Los Angeles, but still following the diet that had worked for me in India. Now, in a totally different climate and environment, my body needed different things.

Subscribing to the idea that "Ayurveda says no raw foods" is not truly understanding what Ayurveda is. Ayurveda is a living, breathing, ever-adapting science of life. It is not a diet, but rather a multi-functional philosophy that considers the energies of food, the environment, and the individual. In cold, wintery climates, it's not appealing to eat raw foods. However, in a warm, tropical climate, your body *craves* raw foods because of the hot, humid environment. That is Ayurveda in action. True Ayurveda is not a set of rules and laws you must obey. It's looking more deeply at how you feel and at your environment and making food choices that match your needs.

LISTEN TO YOUR DOSHA

The amount of raw foods you need will depend on your Doshic constitution, or mind-body type. There are three Doshas: Vata, Pitta, and Kapha, each with unique characteristics (see pages 40–53). The goal of Ayurveda is to bring the body into balance, and to do this, you need to pacify your primary Dosha with foods that have the opposite quality. For some people, this means raw foods can be a regular part of their diet; for others, it means eating raw foods more sparingly.

As a general rule, if you have a Vata imbalance (feeling cold, dry, bloated, constipated), you should consume more cooked foods because they're warming and easy to digest. However, you can still include some raw foods, like sprouts, in your diet because they can actually rebuild the gut. Raw foods contain more alkaline properties, which can be deeply healing on the digestive system *if and only if* they can be digested. If your Vata increases every time you eat them and you feel out of balance, then consume less. If you feel energized and full of vitality, consume more. Find your perfect fit. For a Vata, I recommend an 80 percent cooked and 20 percent raw diet.

If you have a Pitta imbalance (feeling overheated, oily, acidic, loose stools), you will want to eat both cooked and raw foods, focusing on ingredients such as leafy greens, bitter vegetables, and coconut to cool down your system, alkalize your body, and reduce inflammation. The exact percentage depends on the season, environment, and your unique needs, but Pittas should aim for about 60 percent cooked and 40 percent raw.

If you have a Kapha imbalance (feeling heavy, tired, gaining weight easily, excess mucus), you will want to eat a balance of cooked and raw foods. Cooked foods are easier to digest, but raw foods are lighter and contain fewer ingredients and oils, so they will be better for weight loss and awakening the subtle energy of the body. I recommend a 70 percent cooked and 30 percent raw diet for Kapha.

True Ayurveda is not a set of rules and laws you must obey. It's looking deeper at how you feel and your environment and making food choices that match your needs.

LIVE IN HARMONY

While cooked foods are easier to digest, it's also important to recognize that heating food above 118°F destroys living enzymes, which we need for digestion and *prana*, life-force intelligence. An entirely cooked diet makes many people, including myself, feel heavy and dull, especially in the summer months. Some of us crave more of the pranic life force that exists in raw foods, and many prestigious Ayurvedic doctors, including Dr. Kshirsagar and Dr. Douillard, recommend honoring those needs. Raw foods aren't the problem—it's living out of harmony with your environment. If you live in a place where raw foods are abundant and safely consumed, be one with nature and enjoy them! If you're importing your pineapples from across the planet to your snow-filled city, it's probably not the best choice. Nature naturally provides us with the foods we need—go to your local farmer's market and see what is growing near you. That will give you an idea of what you should be eating.

Chakras

The word *chakra* in Sanskrit means "to wheel." In Ayurveda, this term relates to the wheels of energy within our bodies, from the base of our spines to the top of our heads. Each chakra relates to specific emotional and mental characteristics and can be either excess or deficient, similar to the Doshas. We can use foods, along with lifestyle practices, to bring our chakras back into balance.

SAHASRARA

AJNA

VISHUDDHA

ANAHATA

MANIPURA

SVADHISHTHANA

MULADHARA

ROOT CHAKRA (MULADHARA)
Related to Kapha Dosha and Earth Element

The root chakra is our home-base, relating to the most primitive instinct—survival. It's important we maintain a balanced root chakra so we feel secure and confident in who we are.

A depleted root chakra is extremely common in today's age, as we are disconnected from Earth and spend much more time in our heads than in our bodies. A deficient root chakra will make you feel ungrounded, insecure, or anxious. You may also have weak joints and stiff muscles. These are all Vata-related. Excess root chakra energy may make you territorial and angry, which is Pitta-related.

If you feel that you have a depleted root chakra, try the following tips.

- Consume root vegetables, which have grounding properties, such as sweet potato, carrot, ginger, turmeric, and beets.
- Consume protein-rich, plant-based foods such as nuts, seeds, legumes, and quinoa.
- Consume red foods and spices, such as strawberries, raspberries, pomegranate, beets, tomatoes, paprika, and cayenne.
- Favor cooked food rather than raw food, which is too airy.

SACRAL CHAKRA (SVADISTHANA)
Related to Kapha Dosha and Water Element

The word *svadisthana* means "sweet" in Sanskrit, and this chakra relates to all things sweet: pleasure, love, intimacy, creativity, connection, and passion.

When your sacral chakra is depleted, you cut yourself off from your emotions, seeing them as a weakness. As a result, you may experience sexual dysfunction, skipped menstrual periods, lower-back pain, shallow relationships, communication problems, and fertility issues, which are all Vata related issues. Excess sacral chakra energy may create sexual addiction, which is Pitta-related.

Here are some tips to balance a depleted sacral chakra:

- Consume naturally sweet foods, particularly those that are orange in color: peaches, apricots, mangoes, and sweet potatoes.
- Don't go on a restrictive diet—depriving yourself from the sweet things in life will only further block you from receiving pleasure. Enjoy food without guilt.
- Consume hormone-building seeds such as flax, pumpkin, sunflower, and sesame seeds.
- Consume the Ayurvedic herb *shatavari*, which balances female hormones.

SOLAR PLEXUS CHAKRA (MANIPURA)
Related to Pitta Dosha and Fire Element

Your core is your powerhouse. Not only does it hold you upright, but it also contains your most essential organs. Your solar plexus is your sense of self. It houses your ego (identity), which, to a degree, is necessary to live in the material world.

Those with depleted solar plexus energy will have low self-esteem and lack will-power. They let other people dictate their dreams and visions. Over time, this can lead to digestive issues, back problems, and feeling cold or depleted, which relates to a Vata and Kapha imbalance. Too much solar plexus, however, can make us egotistical and aggressive, which is a Pitta imbalance.

If you feel like your solar plexus chakra is depleted, try the following tips:

- Consume more yellow foods, such as lemons, pineapple, banana, and yellow curry.
- Eat more complex carbohydrates and whole grains, such as starchy vegetables, quinoa, brown rice, oats, and legumes.
- Practice breath of fire, the *pranayama* practice of powerfully and swiftly exhaling to generate heat in the system.
- Spend 20 minutes in direct sunlight each day.

Seed Cycling

Women may want to consider seed cycling to regulate their periods and balance female hormones. Seed cycling integrates various seeds at different points during the menstrual cycle for optimal hormonal balance. Each seed carries specific oils and vitamins to support the body's production, release, and metabolism of hormones.

FOLLICULAR PHASE: Day 1 (start of your period) to Day 14 (or until ovulation), eat 1 tablespoon each freshly ground raw flax seeds and pumpkin seeds daily.

LUTEAL PHASE: From Day 15 (ovulation) to Day 28, (or until menses), eat 1 tablespoon each freshly ground raw sunflower and sesame seeds daily.

HEART CHAKRA (ANAHATA)
Related to Vata Dosha and Air Element

THROAT CHAKRA (VISHUDDHA)
Related to Vata Dosha and Space Element

Have you ever felt this overwhelming sense of love, not for any person or thing but just for life? That's your heart chakra in action. Your heart allows you to see compassion, goodness, and truth in all things. Opening your heart is a lifelong journey that requires daily practice, which is why heart-openers (backbends) are part of every yoga class.

When the heart chakra is depleted, you close yourself to love and connection. You become pessimistic and create excuses to remain in your shell. As a result, you feel constriction in your heart area, suffering from tightness or breathing problems, which are Kapha-related issues. When heart chakra is in excess, you may become overly empathetic and sensitive to other people's energy, which is also Kapha-related.

If you feel like your heart chakra is depleted, these are my tips for you:

- Eat more green foods, such as leafy greens, green juices and smoothies, fresh herbs, avocado, lime, kiwi, and spirulina. While in the Western world red is the color of love, in Ayurveda it's green!
- Do something you love, whether it's dancing, painting, singing, or writing. Let yourself fall in love with the experience of life.
- Practice self-care rituals, such as *abhyanga* (self-oil massage) and dry-brushing, paired with a warm bath and candles.
- Practice deep breathing with your hands on your heart.

The throat chakra relates to all forms of communication, both speaking and listening. When the throat chakra is balanced, we are able to put our thoughts and emotions into words.

When your throat chakra is depleted, you may have a difficult time expressing your truth. You may be fearful of public speaking and afraid of being seen or heard. When you have something that needs to be said and you don't express it, you often experience a lump in your throat. Over time, this can manifest as jaw tightness, strep throat, or thyroid disorder, all of which are Kapha-related. When throat chakra is in excess, you may end up talking too much, which is Vata-related.

If you feel your throat chakra is depleted, here are some tips for you:

- Eat blue foods. Consume lots of blueberries, blackberries, and blue spirulina. Tree fruits such as apples, pears, and plums are also great for balancing the throat.
- Consume warm, healing teas, such as those in the Potions chapter, to soothe this chakra.
- Get vocal. Find your medium, whether it's writing, singing, or creating art. Utilize your unique sense of expression and try other forms—even those that may not feel like they come naturally to you.
- Keep a journal. Write about your dreams, goals, fears, challenges, and everything in between. Remain in a constant state of self-reflection.

THIRD EYE CHAKRA (AJNA)
Related to all Doshas and Elements

We have two eyes to see, but a third to perceive. Intuition is the strongest superpower one can have. The more in touch we are with our intuition, the more easily we can navigate through life. We can trust our gut sense and see through issues without blocking ourselves with the limited perception of the mind. The third eye allows us to see dimensions most people cannot—the greater reason behind why things happen. We can trust that the universe will pan out as it is meant to and look out for signals on which path to take.

When the third eye is depleted, you may find yourself repeatedly in situations you could have avoided with a better sense of judgement. You may have a tough time reading people or situations. You may be unhappy with where you are in life but not know what caused it or how to fix it. You become stuck in the day-to-day and lose sight of the greater scope of life. You catch yourself judging and comparing yourself to other people and need a constant source of stimulation to feel complete.

If you feel your third eye is depleted, give these tips a try:

- Consume more purple foods, such as purple kale, blueberries, cabbage, grapes, purple carrots, and eggplant.
- Take adaptogenic and brain-enhancing herbs such as ashwagandha, brahmi, and bacopa.
- Meditate every morning and night, focusing on the third-eye center, between your eyebrows.
- Immerse yourself in nature to regain touch with your true nature.
- Practice yoga to lessen the ego and expand into your highest self.
- Follow your *dharma*, life purpose, no matter what those around you say.

CROWN CHAKRA (SAHASRARA)
Related to no Dosha or Element

Have you ever suddenly received a rush of inspiration that almost felt like it came from a higher source, such as a poem or business idea? That was your crown chakra opening, allowing you to receive a universal "download." We are always receiving these messages, but most of the time we are too distracted by our minds to listen. This is why a meditative practice is so important for opening that crown chakra. In order to access this level, all of the other chakras must be in balance.

When your crown is open, you are tapped into a limitless source of inspiration. You know the well of creativity will never dry as long as you are tuned into it. You are connected to a source that is so much more expansive than you.

When your crown chakra is closed, you are unable to seek inspiration from a higher source and you look to others for answers and ideas. You are disconnected from your highest self.

If you feel like your crown chakra could use some opening, here are some tips:

- Practice meditation twice a day, for at least 20 minutes each time. It requires a lot of stillness to tune into this higher sense of wisdom.
- When the downloads come through, be prepared to write, because specific downloads rarely reoccur. Surrender to the act of receiving higher source energy.
- Do what makes you feel expansive. Get lost in the song, in the dance, in the moment.
- Remind yourself of how small you are. Spend time in the magnitude of nature.

Discovering
Your Dosha

Introducing the Doshas

What draws most people to Ayurveda are the three Doshas, or mind-body types: Vata, Pitta, and Kapha. Understanding the Doshas and recognizing them in ourselves can help us satisfy the needs of our minds and bodies and become our highest selves.

WHAT ARE THE DOSHAS?

The word *Dosha* means energy. The Doshas consist of the five elements we experience around us: earth, water, fire, air, and ether (space). These elements come together to create the three Doshas.

These natural elements reflect in our bodies. Fire is hot and powerful, like the digestive system. Water is fluid and cool, like our lymphatic system. Earth is dense and grounding, like our structure. Air is light and moving, like our breath. Ether is the vastness that exists inside us when we still our minds.

No one is entirely one Dosha, but rather we are a combination of all three. Ayurveda is a system of regaining balance, so we always treat the Dosha that is out of balance.

VATA
AIR + ETHER

PITTA
FIRE + WATER

KAPHA
EARTH + WATER

VATA

I like to call *Vata* the wind Dosha because it's exactly like that—cold, dry, light, and ever-moving.

The Vata Body

If you have excess Vata in the body, your body has too much wind energy. What's the first thing that comes to mind? Yes, gas. Your body may produce excess gas due to lack of digestive strength. As a result, you may also suffer from chronic bloating or constipation. For you, it's important to amp up your digestive fire. When there is excess Vata in the system, your body temperature tends to drop. Your friends may be in shorts, but you need a second layer. Excess Vata can also cause hormonal issues, such as amenorrhea or low hormones. Your skin may be dehydrated and hair may be dry and frizzy.

The Vata Mind

Excess Vata energy in the mind causes a tornado of thoughts. You may easily become overwhelmed and have a hard time turning your monkey mind off. This can cause difficulty falling asleep and occasionally anxiety. If this is you, work on increasing your Pitta (fire) and Kapha (Earth) energies to regain balance.

VATAS NEED: grounding, warming, stimulating, building

TASTES TO FOCUS ON: sweet, sour, salty

IDEAL MEAL: warm sweet potato soup with spices

Earth is my body. Water is my blood.
Fire is my heart. Air is my breath.
Ether is my spirit

PITTA

I like to call *Pitta* the fire Dosha because that's what it's like—hot, fiery, powerful, and transformative.

The Pitta Body

If you have excess Pitta in the body, your body has excess heat. In Ayurveda, the word for digestive system is the same as the word for fire, *agni*. Those with excess Pitta have too much heat in their fire, causing heartburn, hyperacidity, and even ulcers. Heat rises, so when that fire tries to make its way out of the body, it shows up on our faces as acne. If you ever have trouble with chronic acne or acidity, then you have a Pitta imbalance.

Those with excess Pitta will always feel hot. The moment they start exercising, they're already perspiring. Their perspiration may have a sharp odor because the body is trying to detox.

The Pitta Mind

A Pitta mind is organized and sharp, but when there is excess, it can erupt into a volcano. Impatience, agitation, and anger are all signs of too much Pitta heat in the system. Pittas often become hangry (hungry and angry) if their meals are late, making everyone around them just as miserable as they are. If this sounds like you, work on increasing your Vata (wind) and Kapha (Earth) energies to regain balance.

PITTAS NEED: cooling, hydrating, soothing, calming

TASTES TO FOCUS ON: sweet, bitter, astringent

IDEAL MEAL: steamed leafy greens with avocado

KAPHA

I like to call *Kapha* the Earth Dosha because it's exactly like that—grounded, soothing, calm, and heavy.

The Kapha Body

If you have excess Kapha in the body, you'll feel low in energy. It may take you a while to truly wake up in the morning and exercise is the last thing you want to do. You may gain weight and retain water easily, especially if you eat excess carbs or dairy. You have a sluggish digestive system and metabolism and may sometimes suffer from mucus buildup, such as coughs, colds, or infections. For you, it's important to stimulate your body through your diet to shake out of your Kapha rut.

When there is excess Kapha in the system, you tend to have cold hands and feet, which may sometimes feel clammy. You may have thyroid issues, which is related to your depletion in the throat chakra.

The Kapha Mind

Excess Kapha energy causes the mind to become slower. You may spend a lot of time reminiscing about the past and have a hard time trying new things. Though you are always taking care of others, you may neglect self-care since you put the needs of others in front of your own. If this is you, work on increasing your Vata (wind) and Pitta (fire) energy to regain balance.

KAPHAS NEED: stimulating, warming, detoxifying, energizing

TASTES TO FOCUS ON: bitter, pungent, astringent

IDEAL MEAL: lentil salad with herbs and leafy greens

Vata
MIND-BODY CHARACTERISTICS

Vata is comprised of air and space energy, commonly referred to as wind. Vata energy is in charge of circulation, and there is a great deal of movement going on in their minds and bodies.

THE VATA BODY
Physical Build
Vata types have a naturally small build, with thin bones and a difficult time gaining muscle. They normally have slender wrists, prominent collarbones, and protruding hips. When Vatas do gain weight, it's typically in their midsections.

Skeletal Structure
Vatas tend to have cracking bones and popping joints that are in constant need of an adjustment. Because Vatas have cold and dry body types, their skeletal structure can become stiff without constant movement and lubrication. This is why for Vatas, movement is medicine. Vatas often have hyper-mobile bodies, making them naturally flexible and great at yoga and dance. However, Vatas also tend to have physical irregularities such as scoliosis, bowed legs, pigeon toes, or turned out hips, which makes them most prone to injury. It's important for Vatas to work on stability and balance.

Skin
Vatas tend to have dry skin and hair, commonly on the thin side. They need constant lubrication and must eat healthy fats and protein to prevent hair loss, eczema, and psoriasis. They sometimes have thin skin and visible veins.

Temperature
Vatas have low body temperature and often feel cold when everyone else is comfortable. Vatas need to consume warming foods and beverages in order to bring their temperatures back into balance.

Appetite

A Vata's appetite varies, just like the wind. Sometimes it's ravenous and other times it's barely present. Vatas prefer grazing throughout the day rather than sitting down and eating a meal.

They love snacking on fruit, salads, smoothies, and other food that make them feel light because they're addicted to the feeling of "lightness" (more on that soon). Vatas struggle with routine and have a difficult time fitting meals into their schedule. Every day may be different in the life of a Vata, so it can be hard to plan out meal times. Vatas are the type of people who may go hours without eating, then realize they're starving and overeat. This weakens their already weak digestion because their bodies do not know when to expect food and how much.

Digestion

Internally, Vata types are prone to accumulation of air, leading to bloating and gas. Because they don't retain water well, they often have dry colons, leading to constipation. They feel overly full and even sick if they eat bread, meat, or fried foods, and often suffer from digestive issues such as IBS (irritable bowel syndrome).

This sensitivity is a double-edged sword. Because a Vata's digestive system is so delicate, they are often the first of their friends to make healthy lifestyle changes, simply because processed food does not sit well in their stomach. They enjoy eating healthy foods, not because they are on a diet, but because their digestive systems cannot handle anything else. However, healthy for a Vata is different than healthy for a Pitta or Kapha. Vatas need more lubrication from their diets than the other Doshas because their internal organs are so dry. Raw foods, such as kale salads and uncooked vegetables, can take a serious toll on a Vata's digestive health because their bodies may not be equipped to break them down.

Vatas can suffer from constipation and require extra moisture from their diets to get things moving in their gastrointestinal tracts. This means more oils, spices, soups, and stews. Raw foods require a great deal of energy for the body to digest. If the digestive system is not equipped to break down these fibrous cell walls, even something that seems healthy, like a salad, can become rancid and spread toxicity within the body. Odorous flatulence is a sign of fermentation within the gastrointestinal tract. Bloating after a meal is another sign that the digestive system is working too hard to break down the food.

Lightness

Because Vata is wind energy, Vatas can become addicted to the feeling of lightness. They are the most likely to go on a fast or juice cleanse even though they're the last ones who need it. This desire for lightness also makes Vata types most likely to suffer from eating disorders. They often see mind over body and try to detach themselves from physical needs, such as hunger. As a result, menstrual irregularities are common among Vatas. Vatas tend to be diet "experts," but they aren't always in the best health because they follow what they read instead of listening to their bodies. Vatas must seek balance from within, and strive for regularity in their diet, lifestyle, and exercise routine.

Movement

The word "Vata" means "to move," and that's something Vatas love to do! Vatas feel most alive when they're moving their bodies, whether it's dance, running, yoga, walking in nature, or anything that lets them get out of their chair. They don't do well in desk jobs simply because they can't sit in one place for too long and easily become restless. Vatas perform best when they have the freedom to change sceneries whenever needed.

Energy

A Vata's energy varies just like their appetite; sometimes extremely strong, and other times incredibly weak. Because Vatas love movement, they often overwork themselves to the point of fatigue. Vatas often have extreme, all-or-nothing personalities, and may go from exercising every day to injuring themselves and being forced to take months off.

"If a person doesn't understand themselves, they can't understand anything around them."

—PATANJALI SUTRA

THE VATA MIND

The Vata mind is creative, individualistic, and expansive. They are multidimensional thinkers who love a good conversation. The Vata mind is often idealistic, committed to making the world a better place. Ideas circulate through a Vata's mind like the fall wind, but sometimes it's difficult to organize the tornado going on in their head.

Vatas tend to overthink and overanalyze situations. The hardest thing for a Vata to do is to turn off the chatter in their minds and just get into their bodies. Vatas talk quickly, and their mouths may struggle to keep up with their thoughts. Vatas are full of great ideas, but they may abandon them just as quickly as they come up with them. They may be very passionate about one project only to become overwhelmed by its enormity and completely abandon it before its completion.

Vatas have so many gifts to share that they sometimes don't know which to follow through with. Nature, art, music, dance, and human interaction inspire Vatas and they're happiest when they're around these things. Vatas are not afraid of emotions and can often go places where most people are afraid to. They make great therapists, space holders, and community builders because they are able to connect with the larger vision.

Vatas can be both introverted and extroverted. They're highly social people but also need time on their own to recharge. If they're around people for too long, they can become overwhelmed and shut down. Crowded areas and loud sounds can overwhelm Vatas, such as public transportation and airports. Cold weather and air conditioning also mentally unsettle Vatas, making them feel inexplicably stressed or moody.

Vatas are inspired to create something larger than themselves and experience all there is in life. The Vata mind is aware of the greater consciousness out there and desires to connect with their higher self.

When in balance, Vatas are social, inspiring creators with a strong vision for the future. When out of balance, Vatas become easily overwhelmed, giving up on projects they were once so passionate about. Vatas must focus on one task at a time, so they can finish what they have begun.

Pitta
MIND-BODY CHARACTERISTICS

Pitta is comprised of fire and water, representing transformation. Fire and water are two powerful energies, and Pitta is just that. Pitta is in charge of metabolism, digestion, nutrient assimilation, and more.

PITTA BODY

Physical Build

Physically, Pittas have medium builds with a tendency to become muscular. They have normal body shapes and gain weight evenly throughout their bodies. They have fast metabolisms and are naturally athletic. They tend to have strong jaw lines and more masculine features.

Skeletal Structure

Pittas have normal skeletal structures—neither big boned nor small boned, but somewhere in between.

Skin

Pittas tend to have more oily, sensitive skin that is prone to acne, discoloration, and inflammation. They easily get rashes and hives, and their stress immediately shows in their face.

Temperature

Pitta types contain a great deal of heat energy that needs to be released. They often exhibit signs of fire such as warm hands and feet; burning sensations in the stomach, eyes, or skin; red tones in their hair; or a red, flushed face. They become overheated easily and cannot tolerate hot, humid days. They perspire more than the other Doshas and can have foul-smelling odor from toxic accumulation. They often wake up in the middle of the night feeling overheated, which is why they often need air conditioning.

Appetite

Pittas have strong senses of hunger and thirst and become extremely irritable if they skip a meal. No fasting for them! Pittas need to have their meals on the dot and definitely couldn't go the entire day without eating—plus, people around them wouldn't hear the end of it! For them, food is fuel and they truly suffer without it.

Digestion

Pitta types have the strongest digestion of the Doshas, which gives them their large, sometimes insatiable appetites. However, because their digestions are so strong, they think they can eat anything and feel fine, which is not always the case. Pitta types may get away with consuming unhealthy foods for a while, but after years it adds up, causing hyperacidity, heartburn, and ulcers. Pittas sometimes suffer from loose stools or superfluous stomach acid due to indigestion. As a result, their stomachs release too much acid, leading to heartburn, stomach ulcers, and hemorrhoids.

Pittas are naturally attracted to stimulants such as spicy food, chocolate, caffeine, and alcohol, which further throw them off balance. Pittas should consume more cooling, simple foods, but they often find these to be boring.

Toxicity

Because every cell is created through the Pitta Dosha, Pitta types are the most sensitive to toxicity. This causes digestive issues, sensitive skin, allergies, heartburn, ulcers, and other symptoms of a Pitta imbalance. It is especially important for Pittas to consume organic diets because processed foods and GMOs linger in their systems, even causing toxic emotions such as jealousy, impatience, and hatred.

Movement

Pittas love a good workout, especially when it involves an element of competition, like boot camps or weightlifting. They have a great deal of energy that needs to be released in a positive way and can feel agitated on days they do not exhaust their physical bodies. Pittas tend to enjoy intense exercise to the point of exhaustion.

Energy

Pitta types have intense energy for short bursts of time. They are great sprints, power lifters, and interval trainers. They can work hard for several hours, but need some rest and relaxation afterward. It's important for Pittas not to overwork themselves, which can lead to mental and physical stress and exhaustion.

PITTA MIND

The Pitta mind is ambitious, driven, and goal oriented. They're task-oriented realists who will do whatever it takes to get the job done. Pittas are excellent entrepreneurs and managers who think well on their feet. They love challenges and can become bored if things become too easy. They are sharp-witted and outspoken, and do well in positions of leadership.

Pitta types are driven hard workers who thrive in competition. Their high levels of motivation can make them extremely hard on themselves, leading to burnout, impatience, or anger. Some people can find them intimidating due to their intensity, though they mean well. Pitta types are more realistic than creative. They prefer to actually get something done than to daydream about possibilities. However, sometimes they can get stuck in their own ways and not take other people's suggestions seriously.

They are perfectionists who equate their self-worth with what they are able to accomplish. This creates a never-ending cycle of expectations that often cannot be met by themselves or others. They constantly feel let down by others because they have not matched the high standards they've set for themselves. When the going gets tough, the Pitta gets going. They work well under pressure and will go into overdrive to get the job done.

Pittas are very communal and love feeling like part of something larger than themselves, whether that's a team, school, group of friends, company, or culture. They're often group leaders because they do such a great job in building community. Pittas are motivated by creating change and aren't afraid of the hard work that goes behind it.

When in balance, Pitta types are powerful, achievement oriented leaders capable of great things. When out of balance, Pitta types are irritable, overly competitive, and impatient perfectionists who have difficulty finding satisfaction. Pittas must focus less on external achievement and more on internal peace.

Healing Mantras

Mantras are used to penetrate the unconscious mind and heal the body. When spoken, your tongue presses specific points in your mouth that stimulate the hypothalamus, thalamus, and pituitary glands, healing the mind and body.

Om Sri Dhanvantre Namaha
(om shree don-von-trey na-ma-ha)

Translates to, "Salutations to the being and power of the Celestial Physician." Chant while concentrating upon any condition that you would like remedied or healed.

Om Eim Hrim Klim Chamundayei Vichei Namaha
(om eem hreem kleem chah-moon-dah-yei vee-cheh nahm-ah-ha)

For radiance, confidence, and inner strength.

Om Hum So Hum
(om hum so hum)

Balances masculine and feminine and focuses their combined force.

Hung Vajra Peh
(hoong vahj-rah pay)

Clears out negative thoughts or emotions.

Om Gum Ganapatayei Namaha
(om gum ga-na-pa-ta-yay-a na-ma-ha)

Removes obstacles and resolves conflict.

Om Grinihi Suryaya Adityom
(om grih-nee-hee soor-yah-yah ah-deet-yohm)

Calls the power of the Sun to heal the eyes.

Om Ram Ramaya Namaha
(om rahm ra-my-ya na-ma-ha)

Clears the solar current (down the right side of the body) and lunar current (down the left side of the body) energy paths in body.

Aham Prema
(ah-ham pray-ma)

Translates to, "I am Divine Love."

Kapha
MIND-BODY CHARACTERISTICS

Kapha is comprised of earth and water energy, making them cool, moist, and heavy. Those with high levels of Kapha are calm and settled, and often feel cold or heavy. Kapha is highest in our childhood years, though it can persist throughout our lives, especially in the cold, wet months in winter and early spring.

THE KAPHA BODY

Physical Build

Kapha types tend to gain weight easily and have a naturally curvy, sturdy build. Kaphas tend to have big eyes and round, baby-like faces. Kaphas have the strongest endurance of all three Doshas and can persist for the longest amount of time. When in balance, Kaphas can have a great, strong figure, but when out of balance, they are prone to excess weight. Obesity is a symptom of a Kapha imbalance, caused by too much grounding and not enough movement. Kapha types tend to put on weight in their lower bodies and arms.

Skeletal Structure

Kapha types are naturally bigger boned. Their skeletal structures are sturdy and steady. They have strong bones with well lubricated, stable joints. They are the least likely of the Doshas to become injured.

Skin

Kapha gives moisture to the body, providing them with well-moisturized, soft, supple skin. Their skin retains water and their body holds onto oil, which also gives them luscious, thick hair. However, when out of balance, Kapha types can have combination skin, with an oily T-zone and dry cheeks.

Temperature

Kapha types tend to be on the cold side, as they lack fire energy. They have poor circulation and often have frigid hands and feet. While Vata is cold and dry, Kapha is cold and moist, so their palms may be on the clammy side.

Appetite

Kapha types love to eat, though they do not actually have strong appetites, like Pittas. For them, eating is more for comfort or entertainment, rather than actual physical hunger. They often eat when they are bored, lonely, or frustrated. Kapha types can easily skip meals and may benefit from fasting. They do best eating two meals a day, rather than multiple meals throughout the day, because their bodies take a longer time to digest.

Digestion

Kapha types have a slow digestive system, making them feel full or sluggish for hours after a meal. They are attracted to rich, creamy, heavy foods, like dairy and desserts, because these have similar characteristics to Kapha energy—cold and moist. Fasting is very beneficial to help detoxify excess Kapha, as it provides detoxification and gives digestive organs a chance to rest.

Because Kapha types are naturally so sturdy, their bodies don't require a great deal of protein—in fact, too much protein will actually cause them to gain weight. Kaphas do best on a vegetarian diet.

Heaviness

Kaphas tend to hold onto things—fat, emotions, possessions, the past. They store negative emotions as body weight because of their inability to let go. This fat further grounds their bodies, making them unable to change. Kapha types hold onto water, making them prone to water retention, bloating, and heaviness. They do best when they only drink when thirsty and avoid salty foods in order to not further cause water retention.

Movement

Kaphas move slowly and want to stay in bed for a long time after waking up. They feel resistant to exercise because their bodies are naturally sedentary. However, Kapha types require daily stimulation through exercise, new activities, and change of scenery. It's important for Kaphas not to oversleep, which can sometimes lead to depression.

Energy

Slow and steady wins the race! Kapha types have slow-burning but long-lasting energy. They are very patient and can spend hours on tasks that would leave the other Doshas burned out. They often times feel tired throughout the day, even when they first wake up, and can sleep for hours.

THE KAPHA MIND

Kapha types are pleasant, calm, good-natured people who can easily get along with anyone. They have great ears and are wonderful listeners and advice givers. Kapha types avoid drama, which truly stresses them out and takes a physical toll on their bodies.

Kaphas prefer steady, lasting friendships and relationships and do not like putting themselves out of their comfort zones. They would rather stay at home and be comfortable then go out and risk not having a good time. They don't have a strong need for adventure and challenge and are happiest when they are at peace. They love beaches, hammocks, and, of course, their beds.

They are funny, loving, and have a sweet tone to their voice that naturally draws people. A Kaphas voice is believed to sound like honey, sweetly warming their words with pleasant flavor. They are likable, loyal, and brighten the days of those around them. However, Kaphas often have trouble opening up to others in the way that others open up to them.

Kaphas often suppress their emotions because they feel like they have to play the supporting role for their friends and family. They think if they don't hold it together for everyone else, the world will fall apart. They don't want to hamper other people with their burdens, so they keep problems to themselves and are subsequently left feeling lonely and unheard, though they'll mask it with a smile.

Though their friends may not know, Kaphas are often sad on the inside. Because Kapha is comprised of Earth energy, it is very stagnant and dense. Kaphas similarly may feel "stuck" and lack motivation to make change in their lives. Their endurance can sometimes work against them, as they may continue to deal with a problem, like a bad job or relationship, rather than take a stand in order to change it.

Kaphas often retreat into solitude and may have feelings of loneliness or a longing for the past. They may replay difficult experiences in their minds and wonder what they could have done differently, even when it was not their fault. They are extremely sensitive beings and even a small comment can truly hurt them. Depression is a telltale signal of a severe Kapha imbalance, leading to further solitude, loneliness, and overeating.

Of the Doshas, Kapha types are most prone to self-indulgent behaviors, such as overeating, overspending, and laziness. They are the most likely to binge eat, as they often take their emotions out on food. Many Kaphas are overweight because of this emotional dependency on food. These extra pounds cause not only physical heaviness, but also mental weight. Kaphas often hold on to the past and are unable to create positive change, even when they know it's necessary. They may feel discouraged about starting a workout routine or healthy regimen because they've failed so many before, and end up quitting before truly giving it a chance.

Kapha types often have a tough time speaking their mind, leading to physical imbalances in the throat chakra, which is in the throat region. According to Ayurveda, the mind and body are related, therefore depletion in the throat chakra may manifest in the form of mucus and coughs. Kaphas commonly "swallow their words," which is believed to be related to their congestion and clogged throats. Activities that help open the voice, such as singing, writing, and public speaking are great methods to help counterbalance this depletion.

A Kapha's patience and endurance can help them in many ways as well. They are great at detailed work and make excellent artists, graphic designers, musicians, and chefs. They are loving and giving, naturally attracting people with their sweet disposition. They make wonderful friends and spouses, who are always attentive to the needs of those around them. When Vatas become frazzled and Pittas become angry, Kaphas persist and are able to make it through complicated issues while keeping their cool. As long as they maintain motivation, they are capable of amazing things.

When in balance, Kaphas are calm, content, and stable individuals who can bring people together with their amiable nature. When out of balance, Kaphas can become lazy, self-indulgent, depressed, and resistant to positive change. Kapha types must focus on attending to their own needs as much as they attend to their friends and family. If they constantly give, they can end up feeling emotionally depleted, leading to binge eating, loneliness, and depression. Kaphas are loving people who want the best for everyone, but the most important person they should learn to love and care for is themselves.

"If you don't take care of your health today, you will be forced to take care of your illness tomorrow."

—DR. DEEPAK CHOPRA

What Dosha Are You In the Kitchen?

Now that you know a little bit about the Doshas, let's see which you are in the kitchen!

1. IT'S ALMOST DINNER. WHAT ARE YOU GOING TO EAT?

a The meal I meal-prepped, of course!

b Hmm, no idea… Good question…

c One of the go-to recipes I always make.

2. YOU'RE ABOUT TO PREPARE A MEAL. HOW DO YOU BEGIN?

a I take out all the ingredients I need and measure them out into containers so they're all set when I begin cooking. The French call it *mise en place*, and I call it a lifesaver.

b Turn on some music and start cooking! I'm not even sure what the end result will be, but I'm feeling the flow! I'm snacking the whole way through and most of the time am not even hungry when I'm done.

c I chop up all the vegetables, take out the few ingredients, and put them in my trusty appliances. I prefer simple, easy recipes that are sure to please.

3. HOW DO YOU TEND TO USE COOKBOOKS?

a I follow recipes precisely because I want to make sure I get the right results.

b I look at them for inspiration then kinda do my own thing. I'm a very creative chef.

c I'll try a few recipes that sound like they'll definitely come out well, sticking to ingredients I normally use.

4. HOW ARE YOUR CABINETS ORGANIZED?

a Everything is put into their own containers and labeled. I like to know where everything is so my time spent cooking is efficient.

b All over the place. I tend to leave things in random corners and can never find anything. Organization is not my forte.

c It's relatively organized—I know where all my staples are. However, there are probably some things in the back that have been there for a few years.

5. WHAT KIND OF FOODS DO YOU CRAVE?

a Curries, Mexican, tomato sauce, Thai—anything spicy and with onion and garlic.

b Light snacks, dips, salads, smoothies, chips—I prefer small bites to heavy meals.

c Cheese, bread, pasta, desserts—anything sweet, creamy, or carby.

MOSTLY A: YOU'RE A PITTA CHEF.

You're organized, disciplined, and in control of your kitchen with the mind of a Michelin Star chef. You like to follow recipes precisely to ensure good results. You make the most of your time in the kitchen and like to get in and out of there quickly, while still producing quality meals. You see great value in spending time preparing prior to cooking so you don't have to waste time looking for ingredients or chopping up extra veggies while in action. There is a formula to good food and you like to follow it!

MOSTLY B: YOU'RE A VATA CHEF.

You're the creative type that lets the food move you. You often begin cooking with no idea what the end result will be and like it that way. You can't even remember a time you stuck to a recipe precisely. To you, food is all about bending rules and finding your own unique flavor. Each time you enter the kitchen, something new comes through and you wouldn't have it any other way. Even if it's not perfect, you still enjoyed the process…though you do burn your food more often than you'd like to admit.

MOSTLY C: YOU'RE A KAPHA CHEF.

You're a chef of comfort that likes to stick to what they know—after all, if it tastes good, why change it? You have your go-to recipes that your entire family loves and can basically reproduce them on autopilot. Your multi-cooker is your BFF and you aren't a fan of using fancy ingredients or spending extra time plating a meal. Taste triumphs appearance and sometimes the simplest foods are the most delicious…especially with some extra creaminess.

What Do I Eat?

Once you get cooking, make the foods that will bring your body into balance.

VATA: Eat more warm, cooked, grounding meals. Stews, curries, roasted veggies, and soups are their jam. Dry, cold foods like popcorn, crackers, or excess raw foods will throw a Vata off balance, causing bloating, gas, and anxiety.

PITTA: Eat more cooling, detoxifying meals: leafy greens, juicy fruit, simple grains, steamed vegetables, and protein-packed legumes. Spicy and pungent foods like tomato, onion, garlic, and meat will knock Pittas off balance, causing acidity and impatience.

KAPHA: Eat more stimulating, light foods. Bitter vegetables, leafy greens, spices, and herbs are perfect for Kaphas. Oily and heavy foods like dairy products, excess carbohydrates, fats, wheat, and sweeteners will cause them to gain weight and become sluggish.

Multiple Doshas

You might be wondering, "What if I relate to multiple Doshas?"
Have no fear—that's totally normal! In fact, we are all a
combination of the three Doshas, just in varying amounts.

DUAL DOSHAS

Most people have two prominent Doshas, a primary and
a secondary one. Sometimes we alternate between the
two, while other times we display characteristics of both
at the same time. Everybody has the tendency to sway
toward one Dosha or another because we live in an
ever-changing world that is constantly knocking us off
balance. It is up to us to reassess our diet and lifestyle to
make sure we are best serving our bodies' current needs.

TRIDOSHAS

Many people believe they are tridoshic because they can
relate to all three Doshas. However, being truly tridoshic
is extremely rare and is called *sama dosha prakruti*, meaning
"perfect health." Although you may relate to all three
Doshas, this is just because there are varying degrees of
each Dosha in all of us; it does not mean you are
completely tridoshic.

DUAL DOSHA CHARACTERISTICS

VATA-PITTA

- Generally thin like a Vata, but with better stamina
- Goal-oriented like a Pitta with the ideas of a Vata
- Perfectionists—both Doshas make them very hard on themselves
- Creativity of a Vata with the focus of a Pitta
- Less indecisive than pure Vata types
- Less competitive than pure Pitta types
- Stronger digestion than pure Vatas
- Tolerate cold better than pure Vatas

PITTA-VATA

- Medium build like a Pitta
- Less scrawny than a Vata but may not be as athletic as a Pitta
- Stronger digestion than a Vata, less prone toward bloating
- Pitta energy makes them able to tackle problems without becoming overwhelmed like Vatas
- Under stress, may become irritable like a Pitta or tense like a Vata
- Tolerate heat better than Pittas and cold better than Vatas

"When something seems to change in the world, the rishis said, it is really you that is changing."

—DR. DEEPAK CHOPRA

PITTA-KAPHA

- Athletic like a Pitta while sturdy like a Kapha
- More sturdy than Pitta-Vatas
- Less indulgent than a Kapha, and more ambitious
- Pitta and Kapha energies make them VERY agitated if they skip a meal
- Strong digestion
- Able to handle extreme conditions and remain collected

KAPHA-PITTA

- Muscular build but tendency to gain more fat than a Pitta-Kapha
- Rounded face and body like a Kapha
- More easygoing than Pitta-Kaphas
- Enjoy exercise more than Kapha types, with strong endurance
- Less competitive than Pitta-Kapha types
- Sticks to routine, and doesn't like change
- Organized

VATA-KAPHA

- Rarest combination because they are opposites
- Generally Kapha personalities with Vata bodies
- More chill, mellow, and easygoing than a pure Vata
- Can be very small-boned due to Vata imbalance
- Tend to procrastinate—Kapha makes them lazy and Vata makes them flaky
- Dislike cold weather—both Vata and Kapha are cold energies
- Prone toward bloating and slow digestion—both Vata and Kapha are prone toward digestive issues; however, a Vata's bloating comes from excess gas while a Kapha's comes from water retention

KAPHA-VATA

- May have a Kapha body with a Vata personality
- More idealist, artistic, and full of thoughts than a pure Kapha
- Not as settled in times of stress as a Kapha, can get anxious like a Vata
- Stronger stamina than pure Vata types
- Can gain weight more easily than a Vata
- Vata and Kapha energy makes them attracted to sweets for energy
- Doesn't sleep as much as pure Kaphas, and may suffer from insomnia

How Doshas Change
WITH TIME AND SEASON

Your Doshic constitution is not stable; it can shift throughout the year and even with the time of day. Stay tuned in to the changes in your environment to give your body what it needs.

DOSHAS AND THE SEASONS

Each Dosha is associated with a season—Vata is cool and crisp, like fall; Kapha is cold and moist, like winter and early spring; and Pitta is hot and fiery, like summer. To stay balanced, it's important to consume more of the foods that pacify the associated Dosha as you move through each season. This is especially important during the season associated with your primary Dosha, as the weather can cause greater imbalance. However, because we all have elements of all three Doshas within us, we should always strive to balance the qualities of our food with the qualities of the season.

SEASON	SUMMER	FALL	LATE WINTER/ EARLY SPRING
ASSOCIATED DOSHA	Pitta	Vata	Kapha
SEASONAL IMBALANCE	Perspiration, rashes, inflammation, irritability, excess oil	Dry skin, constipation, insomnia, anxiety, bloating	Lethargy, weight gain, oversleeping, water retention, congestion
EAT MORE	Cool, refreshing foods, like watermelon and cucumber	Warming, moist foods, like soups and grains	Warming, light foods, like cooked greens, berries, and warming spices
EAT LESS	Spicy food, coffee, chocolate, alcohol	Dry, crisp foods, like crackers; salads; cold drinks; smoothies	Excess carbs, sugar, dairy, wheat

DOSHAS AND THE TIME OF DAY

Ayurveda splits the day into six 4-hour periods. Each period is related to one of the three Doshas, and repeats twice during the day.

6AM–10AM KAPHA TIME

As the sun rises and Earth slowly wakes up, we enter grounding Kapha time. Eat a light, easy-to-digest breakfast to begin to kindle your digestive fire. I offer warming breakfast variations catered to each Dosha so you can choose the one according to the Dosha you are seeking to balance.

10AM–2PM PITTA TIME

As the sun rises higher in the sky, we enter Pitta time. This is when our digestive strength is at its peak, making it the best time of the day to eat a big meal. Our bodies have woken up and have the rest of the day to break down food, absorb nutrients, and eliminate waste. I recommend consuming a Six-Taste Bowl (see pages 124–151), filled with the six tastes of Ayurveda, to give you all the nutrients you need and prevent cravings.

2PM–6PM VATA TIME

The mid-afternoon lull is far too common because so many people aren't feeding their bodies right. Believe it or not, you shouldn't feel exhausted in the afternoon! It could be a sign that you aren't sleeping enough or getting enough nutrients from your food. Instead of reaching for a second coffee or the office candy stash, try one of my snack recipes, which are chock-full of healthy fats and protein.

6PM–10PM KAPHA TIME

The second Kapha time of day is when the sun sets and we prepare our bodies for sleep. Ayurveda recommends consuming a light, easily-digestible dinner, such as soup or *dhal* (lentils), so our bodies can quickly digest the meal before sleep. However, I understand that for many of us, dinner is the only warm, freshly cooked meal of the day, and for that reason, I offer both my chakra soups as well as more filling meals.

10PM–2AM PITTA TIME

To all my night owls, this is when you get your second wind. As the craziness on the Earth settles, you finally begin to get into your flow. However, this is the most important time to catch some zzz's, as sleep before midnight is the most nourishing for the body. Try to turn off your electronics for two hours before bedtime and practice some self-care rituals, like self-oil massage and dry brushing, to whisk your mind and body into dreamland.

2AM–6AM VATA TIME

This is a sacred time when the veil between the universe and Earth is lifted. These are the hours of the artist, the dreamer, and the spiritual seeker. In Kundalini yoga, practitioners are advised to awaken at 2am to practice their *kriyas,* chanting, because we are more in tune with our higher, universal selves, *atman.* This is the best time for deep sleeping and connecting with the dream world.

Understanding Prakriti and Vikruti

We were all born with a specific Doshic constitution, called our *Prakriti*. Over time, lifestyle and habits can change our Doshas. The Doshic constitution you have today is called your *Vikruti*. In order to reach optimum health, you need to get back to your Prakriti by addressing the imbalances you currently have.

ASSESS YOUR PRAKRITI

Your Prakriti gives you an understanding of what your body is naturally prone toward. If you were born with many Vata traits, you are more likely to suffer from more Vata imbalances, especially during cold and dry seasons. Same goes with all the Doshas. Keep in mind your Prakriti can be a combination of two Doshas (I'm a Vata-Kapha).

As you take this quiz, think of the qualities you naturally have. Answer according to your lifelong tendencies—the you as a child. Check all that apply in each category.

Scoring
MOST CHECKS IN CATEGORY 1
Pitta Prakriti

MOST CHECKS IN CATEGORY 2
Vata Prakriti

MOST CHECKS IN CATEGORY 3
Kapha Prakriti

CATEGORY 1

- When I wrap my hand around my wrist, my fingers exactly touch.
- I am naturally athletic and able to put on muscle if I try.
- I have a competitive streak and love leading.
- My skin is on the oily side, prone to acne and redness.
- I have a reddish tint to my skin and hair.
- I tend to run hot and prefer cool weather.

CATEGORY 2

- When I wrap my hand around my wrist, there is a lot of space left.
- I have long fingers and limbs, prone to injury and cracking.
- I am the creative type and love brainstorming.
- My skin is on the dry side.
- I have thin hair, prone to frizziness.
- I tend to run cold and prefer hot, humid weather.

CATEGORY 3

- When I wrap my hand around my wrist, my fingers do not touch.
- I have always struggled with my weight.
- I have a calm, peaceful demeanor and love working with my hands.
- I have glowing dewy skin, sometimes with an oily T-zone.
- I have thick, lustrous hair.
- I tend to run cool and prefer hot, dry weather.

ASSESS YOUR VIKRUTI

Lifestyle, diet, and age can disrupt your Doshic constitution. For example, let's say you are eating lots of sweets, breads, and dairy, all of which induce Kapha. Then you are likely to suffer from a Kapha imbalance, gaining weight and becoming mucus-y, even though you may not naturally be a Kapha.

As you take this quiz, think of how you feel today. Check all that apply in each category.

Scoring

MOST CHECKS IN CATEGORY 1
Kapha Vikruti

MOST CHECKS IN CATEGORY 2
Vata Vikruti

MOST CHECKS IN CATEGORY 3
Pitta Vikruti

CATEGORY 1

I experience:

- ○ Excess mucus and phlegm
- ○ Weight gain
- ○ Water retention
- ○ Sluggishness
- ○ Slow digestion
- ○ Frequent colds, coughs, and congestion
- ○ Feelings of loneliness or depression

CATEGORY 2

I experience:

- ○ Bloating or gas
- ○ Constipation
- ○ Menstrual irregularities
- ○ Anxiety or insomnia
- ○ Frigidness
- ○ Burnout
- ○ Pale skin

CATEGORY 3

I experience:

- ○ Hyperacidity or heartburn
- ○ Loose stools
- ○ Acne
- ○ Constant or odorous perspiration
- ○ Inflammation
- ○ Red skin
- ○ Irritability

ADDRESSING YOUR IMBALANCES

Your Prakriti and your Vikruti may be two different things. You may be primarily a Pitta, but suffering from a Vata imbalance due to eating too many Vata-inducing foods, like salads and smoothies. Or you may naturally be a Vata but have gained weight and now suffer from sluggishness and water retention, due to your Kapha imbalance. When you are suffering an imbalance, it's important to eat according to that Dosha. This will help offset the imbalance by counteracting it with foods in the opposite quality.

"If you want to see what your thoughts were like yesterday, look at your body today. If you want to see what your body will be like tomorrow, look at your thoughts today."

—INDIAN PROVERB

Eating the Ayurvedic Way

Finding Your Balance

The goal of an Ayurvedic diet is to bring your body into balance and keep your *agni*, or digestive fire, strong. The first step in achieving balance is recognizing what elements are out of balance. Then you can assess the qualities of your food and your environment to determine what your body needs to regain balance and strengthen digestion. You'll find that once you begin striving for balance, your body will naturally crave what you need.

LISTEN TO YOUR BODY

Have you ever noticed that after eating clean for a while, you start craving those veggies and quinoa you once shied away from? One day of eating unhealthy (including foods you used to have no problem with) and your body is practically screaming at you for something green. That's your body trying to get back into balance.

Now have you ever noticed the opposite, after an indulgent weekend full of Friday drinks, Saturday night dinners, and Sunday brunches, it's basically impossible to go back to steamed veggies on a Monday? That's because your body shifted into an imbalance and wants to continue indulging in those highly stimulating empty calories. I like to call this "the law of cravings." You will further crave the foods you regularly put into your body.

KEEP UP THE MOMENTUM

A body in balance will further crave the foods that keep it *in balance*, while a body out of balance will further crave the foods that will knock it *off balance*. The closer your body moves toward balance, the more it will push to keep the momentum going. The more your body is imbalanced, the more it will try to continue with the unhealthy habits. If you are in the middle, it's easy to stray either direction.

When your mind and body are in balance, you are able to make decisions that will make *both* feel better, not just one or the other. Your mind will say, "I feel pretty crappy right now, but last time I felt this way and polished off a tub of ice cream, I felt even worse afterward. This time I'm going to pack up my mat and head to yoga." You'll be able to recall the heavy Kapha slump the ice cream left in your body and mind. Instead you'll choose to sacrifice your immediate happiness to sweat it out a bit and feel the yoga high.

STAY TUNED IN

Once you are in balance, you'll be able to be your own judge. Your mind and body will tell you how much to eat, work, sleep, socialize, exercise, and rest. When you have been treating your body right, you will intuitively know what works for you and what does not. You'll know when you need soup instead of salad, or when you need a piece of chocolate and a cup of tea. The more in touch you are with your body's needs, the better you will be able to nourish it.

IS YOUR DOSHA IN BALANCE?

BALANCED	DOSHA	OUT OF BALANCE
Excitable, creative, imaginative, spontaneous, adaptable	VATA	Bloating, gas, constipation, chills, insomnia, weakness, anemia, malabsorption, PMS, missed/irregular periods, anxiety, lost appetite, nervousness, fatigue
Strong, intellectual, powerful, confident, strong digestion	PITTA	Heartburn, aversion to heat, hyperacidity, red flushed face, acne, anger, irritability, impatience, bossiness, competitiveness
Affectionate, sweet, calm, settled, strong endurance	KAPHA	Asthma, allergies, depression, materialism, possession, jealousy, weight gain, procrastination, fluid retention

The Six Tastes of Ayurveda

In Ayurveda, nutrients are not described in numbers or letters. They're measured in six tastes: sweet, sour, salty, bitter, astringent, and pungent. When you eat a diet filled with the six tastes, you naturally find balance in all three Doshas.

TASTE (RASA)	SWEET (MADHURA)	SOUR (AMLA)	SALTY (LAVANA)	BITTER (TIKTA)	ASTRINGENT (KASAYA)	PUNGENT (KATU)
DOSHA EFFECT	- Vata - Pitta + Kapha	- Vata + Pitta + Kapha	- Vata + Pitta + Kapha	+ Vata - Pitta - Kapha	+ Vata - Pitta - Kapha	+ Vata + Pitta - Kapha
ACTION	Grounding, nourishing, building	Stabilizing	Grounding, hydrating, moisturizing	Cleansing, nutritious	Clarifying, drying, calming	Stimulating, warming, energizing
EXAMPLES	Sweet potato, grains, fruit, oils, avocado	Citrus, apple cider vinegar, tamarind	Sea salt, sea veggies, celery	Leafy greens, brussels sprouts, asparagus	Legumes, sprouts, most raw vegetables	Garlic, mustard, hot spices, onions
BENEFITS	Slows digestion, promotes longevity, improves strength, calms nerves	Improves appetite, increases saliva, improves absorption, supports digestion	Softens tissues, stimulates digestion, balances electrolytes	Cleanses, detoxifies blood, provides magnesium and calcium	Slows digestion, absorbs water, dries fat, tighten tissues	Boosts appetite, stimulates circulation, clears sinuses, stimulates senses

VATA IMBALANCE

Include more sweet, sour, and salty foods

PITTA IMBALANCE

Include more sweet, bitter, and astringent foods

KAPHA IMBALANCE

Include more bitter, pungent, and astringent foods

THE ESSENCES OF FOOD

The sweet, pungent, and salty tastes are favorites of the general population (hello, chocolate, hot sauce, and chips), but the bitter, sour, and astringent tastes are equally important. In Ayurvedic terminology, these six tastes are called *rasas*. Far more than flavor and taste, rasas allude to the essences of our food and the powerful impact they have on our body, mind, and spirit. The rasas alert our bodies of the upcoming effects of the food we're eating so our digestive systems are prepared.

When you skip out on naturally sweet foods like fruits, sweet potatoes, and grains, your body begins signaling for you to eat the sweetest thing possible—which is why you end up in your office's candy drawer at 3pm. We all must consume the six tastes each day to keep our bodies nourished and satisfied, and to prevent cravings from taking the driver's seat. However, we can adjust the proportion of each taste to balance our particular Doshic constitution.

For an easy, customizable way to get in your six tastes each day, make a Six-Taste Bowl for lunch (see pages 124–151).

Qualities of Food

Ayurveda is focused on the sensation each food creates in your body. The more in touch we are with the effects of each food on our bodies, the more we can create a balanced diet for our bodies' specific needs.

GUIDED BY GUNAS

Ayurveda teaches that there are ten pairs of food qualities used to describe all foods. These qualities are called *gunas*, and they can be thought of as the sensation or energy that food brings to the body. The gunas are grouped in opposing pairs that balance one another, such as heavy and light or hot and cold. Considering the gunas allows us to counterbalance our environmental and internal states by consuming foods with the opposite qualities.

For example, if you are in a hot and dry desert, what your body needs are the opposite qualities, such as a cool, hydrating coconut water. If you are feeling heavy, cold, and sticky, it would be best to refresh the body with something light, warm, and stimulating, like ginger tea. Becoming aware of these characteristics allows us to assess what foods we should be eating according to the way they will make us feel.

The more in touch you are with the qualities of your food, the more in touch you become with the qualities of yourself. That way you can become your own doctor, prescribing yourself exactly what foods you need to counterbalance your current state. Let these gunas be your guide to assess your body's current state needs and feed it exactly what it needs. Using our meals as medicine, we can achieve mind-body balance, leading to lasting health and radiance.

The 10 Food Quality Pairs

HEAVY VS. LIGHT

When we think heavy foods, we tend to think of things like a rich Thanksgiving dinner, but heavy foods aren't necessarily unhealthy. Heavy foods are often warming and grounding, which is why the body needs them in the cold Vata months. Light foods, on the other hand, keep us uplifted and energized because they require little energy to digest, which is why we need them in the heavy late winter and early spring Kapha months.

HEAVY FOODS: Stews, curries, casseroles, nuts, nut butters, coconut

LIGHT FOODS: Leafy greens, sprouts, cucumber, berries

NOTE: Many dieters make the mistake of only eating light foods, which actually leads to an imbalance. We need a combination of both heavy and light foods to keep our bodies in balance. Too many light foods will make us feel anxious, fatigued, undernourished, and restless, while too many heavy foods will make us feel lethargic, overweight, and depressed.

CATEGORY 2: TEMPERATURE

HOT VS. COLD

Hot and cold don't just relate to the temperature of the food but also the energy you are left with after eating. Heating foods stimulate the *agni*, digestive fire, providing you with internal heat. Your body temperature increases just by consuming them, like taking a bite out of a chile, which is why they're a good choice for Vatas and Kaphas, but not so great for Pittas. Cooling foods bring down the body's temperature, reduce acidity, and lower blood pressure, making them a great choice for fiery Pitta types.

HEATING FOODS: Ginger, turmeric, cayenne, cumin, turmeric, onion, garlic, tomato

COOLING FOODS: Zucchini, kale, broccoli, cabbage, celery, cucumber, coconut water

OILY VS. DRY

In order to gain balance, we require both oily and dry foods. Oily foods make us feel grounded, while dry foods make us feel uplifted. Oily foods do not necessarily need to contain oil but are rather any source of healthy fat, such as avocado and walnuts. Fats allow us to retain moisture, leaving us with beautiful, radiant skin. Without fats, our skin would not be able to hold onto moisture, causing premature aging. Dry foods, on the other hand, make us feel light and agile.

OILY FOODS: Coconut, sesame, avocado or olive oil, avocado, nuts, nut butters

DRY FOODS: Granola, crackers, rice cakes, kale chips

SOLID VS. LIQUID

You may have been prescribed a liquid diet when you were sick. Liquid foods require no energy expenditure for digestion, giving your body more energy to heal itself. However, as soon as you get better, you crave more solid, substantial foods. Solid foods give strength, increase digestive strength, and provide satiety to the mind and body. Even just chewing solid foods burns calories, which is why both are required in an Ayurvedic diet.

SOLID FOODS: Celery, brussels sprouts, tempeh, kale, nuts

LIQUID FOODS: Broths, soups, juices, smoothies

FAST VS. SLOW

The speed of the food doesn't have to do with how fast it was cooked but rather how quickly it's digested. Fast foods, such as simple carbohydrates, give immediate energy to the body, while slow foods, such as proteins, take longer. Eating too many foods that are quickly absorbed can lead to overstimulation and weight gain, while too much food that is slowly absorbed can lead to lethargy and heaviness.

FAST FOODS: Fruit, honey, dates, grains

SLOW FOODS: Tofu, tempeh, beans, nut, seeds, quinoa

STABLE VS. MOBILE

The mobility of the food refers to how changeable the substance is. Stable means static, while mobile means spreading. Stable foods are substances whose properties are not easily changed. An example would be coconut oil, as it can be reheated and cooled down numerous times while still retaining the same qualities and returning to the same nature. Stable foods promote structure in the body, increasing Kapha energy. They promote growth, muscle restoration and recovery; however, too much can be restricting. Mobile foods change drastically; for example, a sprout goes from a seed to a living green. Mobile foods increase our Vata energy, enhancing agility in the mind. However, too much can lead to restlessness.

STABLE FOODS: Coconut oil, grains

MOBILE FOODS: Sprouts, leafy greens

HARD VS. SOFT

The elasticity of the food refers to the firmness of the ingredient. Hard foods provide structure to the body and mind and balance out soft, sedentary Kapha energy. Soft foods, on the other hand, provide comfort and can ease a rigid Pitta mind. Excess hard foods cause inflexibility, while too many soft foods can cause laziness.

HARD FOODS: Nuts, jackfruit

SOFT FOODS: Mashed sweet potato, oatmeal, puréed vegetables, yogurt

CLEAR VS. CLOUDY

The clarity of the food refers to the purity and simplicity of the meal. Clear foods promote emotional and mental clarity, while cloudy foods calm the mind and body. Cloudy foods are richer and contain more ingredients than clear foods, which are very simple. Excess clear foods can cause light-headedness from a lack of grounding, while excess cloudy foods can lead to heaviness and lethargy.

CLEAR FOODS: Vegetable broth, water, coconut water, herbal tea

CLOUDY FOODS: Curry, casserole

SMOOTH VS. ROUGH

The texture of the food is very easy to recognize and can be classified as either rough or smooth. Rough foods, such as raw vegetables, require a great deal of chewing while smooth foods are very easy to digest. Rough foods contain more fiber, and are more detoxifying for the body, as the roughage helps cleanse the colon. However, excess rough food can be difficult for the body to digest and can cause rigidity in the mind and body. Smooth foods promote flexibility and agility in the mind and body. However, consuming only smooth foods can weaken your digestive system, because it requires such little energy expenditure.

ROUGH FOODS: Raw carrot, kale, celery, broccoli, cauliflower

SMOOTH FOODS: Kitchari, avocado, blended soups

SUBTLE VS. GROSS

The structure of the food refers to the way the food is prepared. Think of a salad. The more finely chopped the salad is, the more ingredients you take in with each bite. Chopping a salad increases its subtle quality, as it becomes finer. However, chopping it too finely may lead to overstimulation because there are too many ingredients involved at once. A salad with fully intact pieces of vegetable is more grounding because you are consuming the ingredients the way they were created in Earth. It brings us back in touch with the natural quality of the food, without the refinement. However, eating only full heads of lettuce and carrots will lead to excess grossness, making our palates insensitive. It will also be extremely difficult to digest.

SUBTLE FOODS: Finely chopped foods, spices, herbs

GROSS FOODS: Whole vegetables, roots, tubers

Energies in Food

Just like there are three Doshas—Vata, Pitta, and Kapha—in Ayurveda there are also three cosmic forces, which are the subtler forms of each Dosha—*prana, tejas,* and *ojas.* These energies are present in the foods you eat, and consuming foods that are high in prana, tejas, or ojas can bring those energies into your body.

ENERGY	DESCRIPTION	
PRANA VITAL LIFE FORCE THE SUBTLE FORM OF VATA RELATED TO CREATIVITY, INTUITION, LIGHT, AND AIR	Someone who is high in prana is very energetic, adaptable, and present. They are full of life-force, blissful and loving energy. They breathe calmly and peacefully, and have flexible, fit bodies.	Someone who is low in prana easily becomes stressed out and overwhelmed. They harbor fear-based emotions and frequently become depleted in energy. They tend to have shallow breaths and feel cold or numb in the extremities.
TEJAS SPARK OF RADIANCE THE SUBTLE FORM OF PITTA RELATED TO STRENGTH, PASSION, MOVEMENT, AND FIRE	Someone who is high in tejas has a twinkle in their eyes and particular radiant glow. They're confident, brave, and sharp people, who naturally attract others with their powerful energy. They have shiny eyes, luminous skin, and a brilliant mind.	Someone who is low in tejas tends to lack motivation and drive. They may be fearful of being seen and similarly suffer from weak digestions and sluggish metabolisms. Those with excess tejas, however, will experience heartburn and other Pitta imbalances.
OJAS LUSTER OF LIFE THE SUBTLE FORM OF KAPHA RELATED TO GROUNDING, JOY, STABILITY, AND EARTH	Someone who is high in ojas beams with a shining golden light. They have a warm, welcoming presence and they radiate like the sun, brightening up whatever room they're in. They have smooth, clear, and glowing skin; a strong immune system; and healthy weight.	Someone who is low in ojas doesn't have a healthy appearance. They may look gaunt, weak, or tired, with baggy eyes and puffy skin. They become stressed and ill easily and look like they haven't been taking proper care of themselves.

FOODS HIGH IN THIS ENERGY	BALANCED	OUT OF BALANCE
• Freshly picked—the moment food is picked, it begins losing prana, so it's best to buy local and seasonal food to prevent high food miles • Colorful—foods that look vibrant make you feel vibrant • Pure raw green juices without fruit—the most prana-filled food out there • Sprouts and sprouted nuts and seeds—the sprouting process brings food to life • Blue green algae and sea plants—spirulina, chlorella, kombu, kelp, wakame	• Creative • Enthusiastic • Adaptable • Inspired	• Weak • Anxious • Ungrounded • Disorganized • Overwhelmed • Dull and heavy
• All warming spices—ginger, cumin, asafetida, black pepper, chilies	• Confident • Motivated • Fulfilled • Radiant	• Hypersensitive • Passive • Tense • Stressed • Overly critical • Irritable
• Sattvic foods—fresh, plant-based ingredients, inclusive of the six tastes of Ayurveda • Avocado and plant-based oils • Sweet potato and fresh fruits • Sprouted nuts and seeds • Turmeric, cinnamon, saffron	• Relaxed • Content • Stable • Joyful	• Fearful • Weak • Hyperactive • Heavy • Unmotivated • Lethargic

Vibration of Foods

Everything has a vibration. Have you ever walked into a room where an argument has taken place and picked up on that negative energy? Have you ever gone to a new city and felt totally at home? Have you ever met someone and something about them just gave you bad vibes? This is you picking up on vibrations.

CHOOSE PRANA-FUL FOODS

Just like people and places have a certain vibration, so do foods. All foods have a vibrational frequency that is related to bioelectricity. High vibrational foods make you feel fresh, bright, light, and full of energy, *prana*. They help us reach higher levels of consciousness and better connect with our intuitive, higher selves. We are able to see the world more clearly when our vessels are clear, thus by consuming high vibrational foods, our life path, *dharma*, comes to light.

The vibration of your food creates the vibration of your thoughts, which sets the vibration of your life.

Interestingly enough, a food's vibration is also related to the Ayurvedic *gunas*, or qualities (see page 68), and the modern alkaline food chart (see page 31). Foods with a high vibration are *sattvic*, pure in nature, and create *prana*, *ojas*, and *tejas*—vital life-force, energy, and radiance. They are also those highest on the alkalinity scale. High vibrational foods raise your energetic vibration and assist the body in eliminating cellular toxins.

Foods with a low vibration, on the other hand, make you feel depressive, dull, and heavy. They are *tamasic* and *rajasic* in energy; depleting and aggravating. They also correlate with the most acid-forming foods. When your body's vibration decreases, your immune system weakens, making it susceptible to parasites, bacterial infections, viruses, and candida. These invaders unload many toxins into the body and can lead to other health issues, such as inflammation, thyroid disorders, autoimmune disease, hormone imbalances, liver and kidney issues, anxiety, and depression.

SLOW DOWN AND ENJOY

How we eat is just as important as *what* we eat. Eating in a rushed manner will decrease the vibration of even the healthiest Six-Taste Bowl, while eating in a restful state will increase the vibration of the occasional dessert. That's not to say you can eat fast food every day in a happy state and all will be fine. However, our bodies can handle the occasional treat if we eat it mindfully without guilt or remorse. Our minds play a much greater role in our overall well-being than we ever could have imagined.

FOODS AND HABITS THAT INCREASE VIBRATION

- Whole foods that are organically grown, local, and seasonal: fruits, vegetables, nuts, and seeds
- Preparing your meals foods with love and intention
- Blessing the food and all who made it possible for your nourishment and pleasure
- Consuming your meal while seated, mindfully chewing each mouthful
- Eating until you are two-thirds full, not stuffed

FOODS AND HABITS THAT DECREASE VIBRATION

- Genetically modified, processed, junk or fast foods: anything containing hydrogenated oils (including palm, canola, or vegetable oil), chemical additives, preservatives, dyes, or artificial sweeteners
- Refined carbohydrates, sugar, fried foods, non-organic dairy and meat
- Using a microwave, which kills the living enzymes in food
- Eating past the point of fullness
- Eating when distracted, angry, tense, or upset

Food Allergies and Intolerances

In the past decade, food allergies and intolerances have grown to unprecedented levels. This is due to a rise in leaky gut syndrome, which makes some people unable to produce the appropriate enzymes to break down certain foods. Leaky gut is caused by a buildup of toxins in the system, caused by GMOs, pollutants, household products, makeup, and other toxins in the environment.

If you are allergic or intolerant to a food, remove it from your diet while you build up your immunity and digestive fire. Steer clear of toxic foods, thoughts, and emotions. Remove from your cabinets any chemical-laden personal care products, detergents, cleaning supplies, and pharmaceutical or recreational drugs. Eliminate sugars, refined carbohydrates, fried foods, alcohol, and caffeine from your diet.

Consume a sattvic, high vibration, alkaline diet. Eat your meals with a peaceful state of mind, and practice daily yoga and meditation to foster the mind-body-soul-spirit connection.

Care for All Your Bodies

To eat and feel fresh, you don't just care for your physical body but rather all of your bodies: energetic, mental, soul, and spiritual. We are like human radios, emitting and picking up on frequencies that surround our bodies, which Ayurveda calls *koshas*. There are five koshas, each which correlate with a specific layer of our beings.

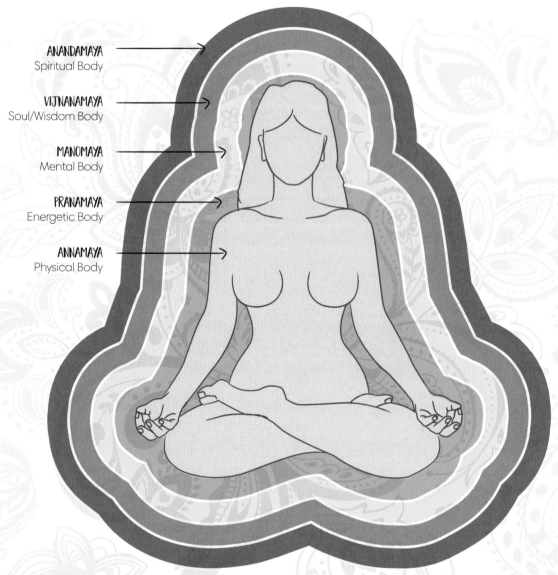

ANANDAMAYA
Spiritual Body

VIJNANAMAYA
Soul/Wisdom Body

MANOMAYA
Mental Body

PRANAMAYA
Energetic Body

ANNAMAYA
Physical Body

CARE FOR YOUR ANNAMAYA KOSHA
PHYSICAL BODY

- Consume a plant-based, sattvic, high vibrational, alkaline diet.
- Practice self-care such as tongue-scraping, dry-brushing, and *abhyanga* (self-oil massage).
- Drink healing teas and elixirs, such as my golden mylk or adaptogenic chai latte.
- Go to bed early and sleep for eight uninterrupted hours each night.

- Practice healthy, empowering, and restorative movement—dynamic vinyasa yoga, restorative yin yoga, long walks, ecstatic dance, strengthening pilates and body-weight exercise, and cooling swimming and tai-chi.
- Spend time in nature each day.

CARE FOR YOUR PRANAMAYA KOSHA
ENERGETIC BODY

- Breathe deeply and slowly—your breath controls your mood.
- Practice *pranayama*, controlled breath meditation.
- Do not engage in media that does not support your growth, such as fear-based news, mindless television, distracting social media, and horror movies.

- Go deep and assess any lingering negative emotions you have been holding on to—fear, anger, pain, sorrow.
- Surround yourself with positive people in an environment that inspires you.
- Stay focused on your own healing—do not try to control or fix others. It will only leave you depleted.

CARE FOR YOUR MANOMAYA KOSHA
MENTAL BODY

- Practice daily meditation to keep control of your thoughts.
- Do not wake up and immediately look at your phone. Keep a one-hour phone-free zone in the first and last waking hour of your day.
- Keep a journal with your thoughts and emotions—try practicing morning pages to let your thoughts flow first thing in the morning and keeping a dream journal.

- Know the difference between your ego self and true self—which desires are yours, and which are placed upon you by society?
- Do something that mentally stimulates you each day—reading, mind puzzles, drawing, activities that require mind-body coordination.
- Don't waste a precious moment worrying about what others think of you and never engage in self-depreciating language.

CARE FOR YOUR VIJNANAMAYA KOSHA
SOUL/WISDOM BODY

- Meditate to access your higher self.
- Get real with yourself—who are you behind the mask? What are your deeper desires? What is your *dharma*, life purpose on this planet? Are you living in alignment with your highest self?
- Spend time on your own in silence.

- Surround yourself by nature's majesty and let yourself be in awe with her perfection.
- Notice the silent whispers of your soul pointing you in the direction of your life purpose.

CARE FOR YOUR ANANDAMAYA KOSHA
SPIRITUAL/BLISS BODY

- Your anandamaya kosha can only be felt when you've balanced your physical, energetic, mental, and soul bodies so make each a daily practice. Self-care is a spiritual practice.
- Practice rituals that connect you with a higher source.
- Allow yourself to experience bliss—smile for no reason at the beauty of life.

- Do things that make you feel alive—dancing, hiking, painting, listening to music, connecting with your true essence.
- Be present in each moment—do not bring the past or future into the moment.
- Know that you are a microcosm of the macrocosm, a child of the cosmos, a piece of the universe in human form, always divinely guided and held.

Eleven Tenets for Health

The recipes in this book are all based on eleven simple principles. Following these guidelines will help keep your *agni* strong, your mind *sattvic*, and your body balanced.

1 EAT FRESH FOODS, STRAIGHT FROM THE EARTH. No preservatives, no MSG, no high fructose corn syrup, and no packaged foods with lots of additives. These foods are the most *sattvic*, meaning they promote mental clarity.

2 AVOID ICED FOODS. Super cold foods, such as ice water and frozen smoothies, will deplete the digestive fire. Instead, sip warm water throughout the day. You can still have smoothies, just avoid frozen produce and include warming ingredients such as ginger and turmeric.

3 CONSUME THE MOST BALANCING FOODS FOR YOUR DOSHA, bringing your *Vikruti* (current Doshic constitution) back into balance so you can go back to your *Prakriti* (Doshic constitution at birth).

- To pacify Vata, consume more warming and grounding foods.
- To decrease Pitta, consume more cooling and hydrating foods.
- To pacify Kapha, consume more light and stimulating foods.

4 ADJUST YOUR DIET SEASONALLY, especially if you live somewhere that undergoes major shifts in weather.

- Consume more Vata-pacifying foods in the fall and early winter.
- Consume more Kapha-pacifying foods in the late winter and early spring.
- Consume more Pitta-pacifying foods in the late spring and summer.

5 NOTICE WHAT GROWS AROUND YOU. Nature produces the types of foods we need for that particular climate and time of year. Eat seasonally and locally, shopping from the farmer's market as much as possible.

PRACTICE THIS AFFIRMATION

I crave the food my body needs. When I tune in, I can trust my body's wisdom.

Your body knows the song of healing. Your mind sometimes just forgets the words.

6 DON'T OVERDO THE GRAINS AND LEGUMES. These can be high on the glycemic-index scale, raising blood sugar and contributing to gut issues and autoimmune disease. Favor non-starchy vegetables instead, such as cauliflower rice instead of regular rice. We live more sedentary lives than we ever have in the past, and consuming a large amount of carbs contributes to weight gain. Make vegetables the center of your plate.

7 CONSUME MORE HEALTHY FATS, particularly those rich in omega-3 fatty acids. Coconut products, avocados, cold-pressed oils, and seeds such as flax, chia, hemp, sesame are great options. Avoid canola or vegetable oil, fried foods, and non-organic animal products.

8 PRACTICE PROPER FOOD COMBINING. Consume fruit on an empty stomach and avoid combining animal products with grains and legumes. If you eat a plant-based diet (avoiding meat and dairy), you easily follow food-combining rules, as most are related to specific ingredients with animal products.

9 AVOID GLUTEN AND WHEAT. Most wheat grown today is genetically modified and can contribute to gluten sensitivity, leaky gut, and autoimmune disease. Even gluten-free wheat products can contribute to these issues.

10 SOAK YOUR GRAINS, LEGUMES, AND NUTS. Soaking breaks down antinutrients in these foods, particularly phytates and enzyme inhibitors, which detract from their nutritional value and make them difficult to digest. Adding cumin, ginger, or mustard seeds to legumes will make them less gas-inducing. A Japanese sea vegetable called kombu is also very effective.

11 AVOID SUGAR AS MUCH AS POSSIBLE. Even natural sugars like honey, maple syrup, and agave, can raise blood sugar levels and feed candida overgrowth. Instead, choose a non-glycemic natural sweetener, such as monk fruit.

The
Eat Feel Fresh
Kitchen

Filling Your Spice Rack

Spices not only add flavor and beautiful color to food, but are also essential for providing healing benefits and balancing the qualities of the meal. These are some of the essential spices in *Eat Feel Fresh*.

TURMERIC

This pungent spice is known for its antiviral, antibacterial, and antiparasitic properties. It purifies the blood, regulates insulin levels (bye-bye, sugar cravings), and protects intestinal flora. Turmeric is a yogi's BFF, decreasing inflammation and helping stretch the ligaments. Turmeric is also the beauty spice, enhancing skin glow and treating acne, eczema, and other skin ailments. It's astringent, bitter, and pungent in taste, but still warming and dry, making it completely tridoshic.

GINGER

Your digestive fire's best friend, ginger helps release toxicity while boosting the metabolism. Ginger is pungent, sweet, and heating, making it tridoshic, though Pittas should not consume it in excess. This spicy root vegetable helps break down proteins and rid the stomach of excess gas. It also improves blood circulation and relaxes muscles, facilitating blood flow throughout the body. Feeling nauseous? Chewing on ginger can help settle the stomach.

ASAFETIDA (HING)

This Indian spice is a powerful digestive agent that will fix any belly issues. It's used to treat bloating, indigestion, gas, and abdominal pain. A little goes a long way—this spice has a strong heating potency that really revs up the digestive fire. If your stomach swells up with air after a meal, asafetida is your cure. This pungent spice also fights candida, balances blood sugar, and helps IBS (irritable bowel syndrome).

CORIANDER

This sweet, slightly bitter, astringent spice releases stored water in the body, great for when you're feeling heavy. Coriander aids digestion, relieves intestinal gas, regulates bowels, and stimulates appetite. It also balances hot and spicy foods, making it especially great for Pitta. It relieves internal heat, excess thirst, acne, rashes, and urinary tract infections. Coriander also promotes liver function, especially necessary if you consume alcohol, caffeine, sugar, or processed foods.

CUMIN

One of the world's most popular spices, cumin is like medicine for digestion. It is bitter, pungent, and astringent—perfect for detoxification, while still being warming to aid digestion. Cumin is used to treat flatulence, bloating, and indigestion. It enhances the digestive fire, improving metabolism and nutrient assimilation. It is a powerful kidney and liver tonic that cleanses your body from impurities. Cumin seeds are also rich in iron and help treat anemia.

CARDAMOM

Sweet, pungent cardamom has heating properties that stimulate digestion and increase nutrient absorption. Cardamom is also a powerful diuretic, helping to shed bloat and water weight. Cardamom clears out the urinary tract, bladder, and kidneys, removing waste, salt, excess water, toxins, and infections. Cardamom benefits all Doshas, expelling gas and undigested food in the colon, relieving acid indigestion and heartburn, and reducing mucus.

SAFFRON

Originally from Northwest Iran, this spice is called the laughing herb because it instantly puts you in a good mood. This sweet, bitter, pungent, and heating spice balances hormones and prevents PMS symptoms. It also regulates blood sugar and aids in carbohydrate metabolism, making it great for healthy weight loss. It also heals acne, purifies the blood, decreases inflammation, and aids in the healthy formation of tissues, bones, and sex hormones.

FENNEL SEED

In India, fennel seeds are chewed before and after meals to prime the digestive system and freshen breath. Fennel is sweet yet slightly pungent and bitter, with light and cooling qualities. Fennel seeds are metabolic enhancers and help boost fat metabolism. They also relieve gas, indigestion, diarrhea, and nausea. Fennel seeds are also used to improve vision, regulate menstruation, prevent anemia, and treat colds.

CINNAMON

Cinnamon has heating, bitter, and pungent qualities, and is a perfect addition to sweet or savory dishes. It stabilizes blood sugar levels, making you less likely to reach for actual sugar, plus slows sugar from releasing into the blood stream, helping manage cravings and weight gain. Cinnamon is also rich in antioxidants, making it great for your skin and disease prevention.

MUSTARD SEED

This pungent spice adds an earthy flavor to salads, stir-fries, and soups. It's anti-inflammatory, antiviral, and antibacterial. It is used to treat parasites, enhance digestion, reduce the frequency of migraines, and even relieve muscular pain. Mustard seeds have heating, oily, light, and sharp properties and make an excellent pungent replacement for onion and garlic for Pittas, yogis, and those with digestive issues.

A NOTE ABOUT
Onion and Garlic

Some recipes in this book include onion and garlic, which have medicinal properties and pungency that can benefit Vatas and Kaphas. However, their pungent flavor is not recommended for Pittas or those on a yogic path (seeking to devote their lives to spiritual enlightenment). If you want to avoid onion and garlic, there are flavorful alternatives to try.

WHEN TO AVOID

Yogis are recommended to consume a purely *sattvic* diet of fresh, plant-based foods. Onions and garlic are *rajasic* in nature for the lower chakras and *tamasic* in nature for the higher chakras, meaning they agitate the body and dull the mind. Science has now found that garlic triggers a mini esophagus spasm, which could be why the ancient rishis stated that it affects our subtle vibration. If you are on a yogic path, try going onion- and garlic-free for several weeks and observe how you feel in your meditation. Go back to them and notice the difference. Most likely, they will overwhelm the senses once you've had some time apart from them.

Pittas are already hot in nature and recommended to avoid pungent and *rajasic* foods, as they can trigger acidity, acne, and inflammation.

Many people today with digestive issues such as IBS (irritable bowel syndrome) and SIBO (small intestinal bacteria overgrowth) also find that they digest much better without onion and garlic. They are both high FODMAP foods, and contain short-chain carbohydrates that are not properly absorbed by some individual's small intestines.

MEDICINAL BENEFITS

This does not mean everyone should avoid garlic and onion. Ayurveda also recognizes the medicinal benefits to both; for example, they are antiviral, antibacterial, and antiparasitic. An Ayurvedic doctor may even prescribe garlic to you if you have a virus as a natural antibiotic. In Ayurveda, everything can be seen as either medicine or poison, depending on who you are and when you eat them.

Onion & Garlic Alternatives

ASAFETIDA

Asafetida (also spelled "asafoetida") is a staple in Indian and Persian cooking because it provides an aromatic flavor very similar to garlic. A little goes a long way, and it's best paired with other spices, such as ginger and cumin. Asafetida prevents flatulence, making it a great choice for adding to cooked beans. Store your asafetida in a tightly closed container, as its powerful aroma can really stink up your kitchen.

REPLACE 1 garlic clove with ⅛ tsp asafetida.

FENNEL

When cooked long enough, fennel loses its licorice flavor and takes on an onion-like taste, making it an excellent, lighter replacement. Simply sauté it in oil until it becomes golden brown along with your favorite spices, such as mustard seeds, cumin, ginger, and fennel seeds.

REPLACE 1 medium onion with 1 medium fennel bulb.

MUSTARD SEED

Mustard seeds are my favorite way to add pungent flavor without onion and garlic. Increase their flavor by toasting them in a hot pan before adding the oil, or heat up the oil and sauté them. Either way, wait until you hear a popping sound, which indicates that the mustard seeds have been activated. Be sure to lower the temperature afterward to prevent them from burning.

USE 1 tbsp mustard seeds at the beginning of your cooking.

CELERY

Celery becomes surprisingly rich, savory, and aromatic when cooked, giving your food flavor and natural sodium while keeping it conscious. I love sautéing celery with cumin, ginger, and ground celery seed.

REPLACE 1 medium onion with 2 celery stalks.

Stocking Your Pantry

In addition to plenty of fresh produce, there are some pantry staples that you'll want to have on hand. These are some of the frequently used ingredients in the *Eat Feel Fresh* kitchen.

NUTS & SEEDS

- Raw nuts and seeds (cashews, almonds, walnuts, chia seeds, coconut flakes)
- Nut and seed butters (sunflower seed, almond, coconut, tahini)
- Non-dairy milk (flax, almond, coconut, cashew)

GRAINS & LEGUMES

- Beans (chickpeas, edamame, black beans, mung beans)
- Brown rice
- Lentils
- Quinoa

Cooking beans from scratch is recommended, but if it's a choice between using canned beans or getting take-out, canned beans win every time!

GLUTEN-FREE HELPERS

- Almond flour
- Arrowroot starch
- Coconut flour
- Ground flaxseed
- Tapioca starch

NATURAL SWEETENERS

- Coconut sugar
- Liquid monk fruit sweetener
- Medjool dates

Pure monk fruit extract is my preferred sweetener because it has no impact on blood-sugar levels and boasts many health benefits.

FLAVOR & HEALTH BOOSTERS

- Adaptogenic herbs (ashwagandha and shatavari)
- Goji berries
- Plant-based protein powder
- Sea salt or pink Himalayan salt
- Spirulina
- Ground vanilla bean

Adaptogenic Herbs

Adaptogens like ashwagandha and shatavari are an important part of Ayurvedic medicine and work synergistically with your body to provide you with exactly what you need. They can help to balance hormones, combat stress, fight fatigue, stabilize blood sugar, treat menstrual issues, increase concentration, and enhance energy.

OILS

Don't fear oils—they're your best friends on your Ayurvedic journey! In fact, in Ayurveda the word for "oil" and "love" is the same, *sneha*. With their digestive-healing, metabolism-boosting, mood-boosting, brain-enhancing, and skin-glowing benefits, oil truly is love.

However, just like lovers, not all oils are created equal. Many common oils such as vegetable and canola are genetically modified, heavily treated with pesticides, and deodorized through chemical processing so they are not what we want in our *fresh* bodies.

Most recipes in this book are cooked and require an oil with a higher smoke point. (A smoke point is the temperature at which an oil will start to burn and smoke, which can create harmful free radicals.) Oils like avocado, coconut, grapeseed, and sesame are recommended for cooking and baking due to their high smoke point, while olive oil works for a light sauté. Flax and hemp oil are best just for drizzling.

Don't buy more oil than you will use in one year. Over time, heat and light can generate free radicals in the oil, which is why it's also important to store them in a cool, dark cupboard or the refrigerator.

Vatas and Pittas should use oil freely, while Kaphas should use it more sparingly. However, Kaphas should not go oil free. Certain nutrients are fat-soluble, meaning fat must be present to properly absorb them. Oils are also the brain's preferred source of fuel, therefore, it's crucial to nourish our brains with healthy fats daily.

Eat Feel Fresh Oil Chart

	SMOKE POINT	CHARACTERISTICS	BEST FOR
AVOCADO	520 °F	Warming, sweet, tamasic, alkalizing	Vata and Pitta
COCONUT	350 °F	Cooling, sweet, sattvic, alkalizing	Pitta and Vata
FLAX	225 °F	Warming, sweet, sattvic, alkalizing	Tridoshic
GRAPESEED	400 °F	Neutral, sattvic, acidifying	Tridoshic
HEMP	330 °F	Cooling, sweet	Vata and Pitta
EXTRA VIRGIN OLIVE	320 °F	Warming, bitter, rajasic, alkalizing	Vata
SESAME	410 °F	Warming, sweet and pungent, sattvic, acidifying	Vata and Kapha

Making It Work

A lot has changed in the 5,000 years since Ayurveda was born. We have refrigerators, making leftovers safe; busy schedules, making meal prep necessary; and appliances that save us hours of time. Make the best of both worlds by combining ancient and modern.

EAT FOR TODAY

Ancient Ayurvedic texts recommend preparing each meal from scratch and serving it immediately, discarding any leftovers because they begin to lose *prana*. However, most of us do not have the luxury to be home all day cooking and serving three meals hot off the stove. We're out of the house working, studying, running errands, and doing all of the other glorious tasks that come with twenty-first century living. For this reason, this well-intentioned Ayurvedic suggestion needs a little tweaking. We have to get with the times and realize that it is better to eat meal-prepped meals than it is to order takeout for lunch.

PREP AHEAD

The most common question I get from people is, "How can I make this work with my busy schedule?" The answer is, plan ahead! It doesn't require setting out a calendar and writing down what you're going to eat each day (though a Pitta may enjoy that process) but just making several large batches of food that you can play with throughout the week. Many of the recipes in this book, particularly the Six-Taste Bowls, start with a base of precooked quinoa, cauliflower rice, or legumes, and roasted or steamed vegetables. Have these on hand, and you're never far from a nourishing meal.

Prepping ahead doesn't have to be time consuming. Setting aside a couple hours each week can mean the difference between healthy homemade meals and last-minute takeout. Twice a week:

- Make a big batch of legumes (add cumin, asafetida, or kombu to make them easier to digest).
- Make a big batch of quinoa, brown rice, barley, or riced cauliflower.
- Roast or steam a big batch of local, seasonal vegetables.
- Make 1–2 dressings to create Six-Taste Bowls.

TIMESAVING TOOL

I recommend purchasing a multi-cooker with the ability to pressure cook, slow cook, and sauté for versatility and ease in the kitchen. Let's say you return from a trip and are famished for a good meal but have nothing in your fridge—you can make a warm lentil soup in just 20 minutes, start to finish. Or suppose you're out of the house all day and want to come home to a warm cooked meal—you can turn on the slow cooker in the morning and come home to a delicious coconut curry, preventing the temptation to order delivery. Pressure cookers are also great for preparing big batches of legumes quickly.

EMBRACE LEFTOVERS

The great thing about Ayurvedic plant-based recipes is that they last covered in your fridge for several days since they do not contain animal products. Though Ayurveda recommends consuming all food warm, if it's a choice between eating cold homemade food versus warm take-out, choose the cold homemade food! At least it doesn't have the additives, salt, canola oil, and inorganic produce served in most restaurants. It's better to eat something cold than to reheat it in your microwave, which diminishes the nutritional content.

USE YOUR FREEZER

Many of my Tridoshic Dinners can be frozen for up to one month and still retain all nutritional benefits. You can also freeze pre-cooked quinoa and legumes and have them easily on-hand and ready to use. It's also the perfect place to stash healthy treats like adaptogenic fudge and bliss balls. Just because freezers didn't exist in Ayurvedic times doesn't mean we shouldn't use them—anything that makes it easier to become healthier while still leading a full life is a YES to me!

	BREAKFAST	LUNCH	SNACK	DINNER
MONDAY	Your Dosha's Om-Meal (p106)	Turmeric Tahini Bowl (p149)	Avocado Tahini Dip (p199) with veggies	Tridoshic Kitchari (p181)
TUESDAY	Your Dosha's Smoothie (p100)	Turmeric Tahini Bowl (p149)	Chai Bliss Balls (p216)	Tridoshic Kitchari (p181)
WEDNESDAY	Your Dosha's Savory Oatmeal (p112)	Thai Buddha Bowl (p128)	Avocado Tahini Dip (p199) with veggies	Sweet Potato Chickpea Burger (p168)
THURSDAY	Your Dosha's Lentil Porridge (p104)	Thai Buddha Bowl (p128)	Fresh fruit	Sweet Potato Chickpea Burger (p168)
FRIDAY	Your Dosha's Chia Pudding (p116)	Goddess Bowl (p136)	Fresh fruit	One-Pot Curry (p165)
SATURDAY	Your Dosha's Quinoa Porridge (p118)	Goddess Bowl (p136)	Tandoori Cauliflower Dip (p202) with veggies	One-Pot Curry (p165)
SUNDAY	Your Dosha's Chai Pancakes (p98)	Sesame Ginger Miso Bowl (p140)	Tandoori Cauliflower Dip (p202) with veggies	Gut-Healing Seaweed Broth (p180)

Basic Prep
FOR LEGUMES, GRAINS, AND VEGETABLES

With precooked beans, grains, and veggies on hand, you're never more than a few minutes away from a healthy meal. Here's how to prep the ingredients you need for Six-Taste Bowls and more.

LEGUMES

Choose organic legumes from a place you trust to ensure they are free of debris, stones, or molded legumes. Cooked beans can be refrigerated in an airtight container for 3–4 days or frozen for 2 months.

Soak

1 Rinse the legumes in a colander under cold running water. Discard any floaters or broken legumes.

2 Place the legumes in a large bowl and add warm water to cover by several inches. To improve digestibility, add 2 tbsp acid (lemon juice or apple cider vinegar) per 1 cup legumes.

3 Soak overnight, around 12 hours. Drain and rinse thoroughly in a colander before cooking.

Cook

1 Place soaked legumes in a pot and add water according to legume variety (see chart). I recommend adding piece of kombu, a Japanese sea vegetable that neutralizes gas-producing compounds in legumes.

2 Cover and bring to a boil, skimming off any foam that rises to the top.

3 Reduce the heat and simmer for the given cook time (see chart). When cooked, legumes should be tender—soft but not mushy.

4 Remove from the heat and leave covered for 1 hour to soften further.

VARIETY	WATER:BEAN RATIO	COOK TIME	COOKED QUANTITY OF 1 CUP DRIED AFTER SOAKING
ADZUKI BEANS	3:1	1½ hours	3 cups
CHICKPEAS (GARBANZO BEANS)	4:1	1½ hours	3 cups
LENTILS, BROWN OR GREEN	2:1	30 minutes	3 cups
LENTILS, RED	2:1	15 to 20 minutes	3 cups
MUNG BEANS	3:1	45 minutes	3 cups
BLACK BEANS	4:1	1 hour	3 cups
SPLIT PEAS	3:1	45 minutes	2½ cups

ROASTED VEGETABLES

This method works well for almost any type of veggie. The smaller the dice, the faster they will cook. Refrigerate for up to 5 days.

3 cups diced vegetables (those with tough outer skins, like squash, should be peeled)

1–2 tbsp sesame, coconut, grapeseed, or avocado oil

1 Preheat the oven to 400°F. In a medium bowl, toss the veggies with oil and mix until well coated.

2 Spread on a rimmed baking sheet in a single layer and bake for 20–35 minutes or until soft and beginning to brown at the edges.

ROASTED BUTTERNUT SQUASH

This is a quick method to prepare squash if you don't want the hassle of peeling and dicing it. Refrigerate for up to 5 days.

1 butternut squash, halved and seeded

1 tbsp sesame, coconut, grapeseed, or avocado oil (optional)

sea salt and freshly ground black pepper

1 Preheat the oven to 400°F. Place squash, cut sides down, in a 9 x 13in baking dish. Pour water into dish around squash halves.

2 Bake until tender and easily pierced with a fork, 25–30 minutes. Carefully remove the skin with a fork. Drizzle with oil, if desired, and season with salt and pepper to taste.

BAKED SWEET POTATO

To make a whole baked sweet potato, or for mashed sweet potato, use this method. Refrigerate for up to 5 days.

2 large sweet potatoes

1 Preheat oven to 425°F. Scrub the sweet potatoes and pat them dry with a towel. Pierce the skin several times with a fork.

2 Place the sweet potatoes on parchment-lined baking sheet and bake for 45 minutes until tender and easily pierced with a fork. Scoop the flesh from the skins for recipes that call for mashed sweet potato.

GRAINS

Buy quinoa and rice in bulk to keep costs down. Cooked grains can be refrigerated in an airtight container for 4–6 days or frozen for 6 months.

1 Rinse the grain well in a mesh strainer. Bring the water to a boil over high heat (see chart).

2 Stir in the grain and turn the heat to low. Simmer for about 15 minutes until all the liquid is absorbed.

3 Let sit for 5–10 minutes, covered, before serving. Use a fork to fluff.

VARIETY	WATER:GRAIN RATIO	COOK TIME	COOKED QUANTITY OF 1 CUP
QUINOA	2:1	15 minutes	3 cups
BROWN RICE	3:1	30 minutes	2½ cups
BARLEY	3:1	30 minutes	2½ cups

EAT FEEL FRESH
Dressings

Homemade dressings are easy to make and free of the stabilizers and sweeteners found in store-bought versions. Plus, they're a great way to deliver sour, salty, and pungent flavors to a Six-Taste Bowl.

ITALIAN

MAKES 6 TBSP

1 tbsp olive oil
2 tbsp apple cider vinegar
juice of 1 lemon
1 tsp Dijon mustard

½ tsp Italian seasoning (oregano, basil, thyme)
pinch of sea salt and black pepper

In a small bowl, whisk together all ingredients. Taste and adjust seasoning as desired. Refrigerate in an airtight container for up to 5 days.

MEDITERRANEAN

MAKES 4 TBSP

2 tbsp freshly squeezed lemon juice
1 tbsp pomegranate molasses (optional)

1 tbsp olive oil
¼ tsp ground cumin
⅛ tsp ground allspice
pinch of sea salt

In a small bowl, whisk together all ingredients. Taste and adjust seasoning as desired. Refrigerate in an airtight container for up to 5 days.

CUMIN LIME

MAKES 6 TBSP

¼ cup lime juice (from about 2 limes)
¼ tsp sea salt
1 tbsp extra virgin olive oil
1 tsp ground cumin

1 garlic clove, minced
1 tbsp minced jalapeño
¼ tsp chili powder

omit for Pitta

Place all ingredients in a jar with a tight-fitting lid and shake vigorously until well combined. Refrigerate in an airtight container for up to 5 days.

ALMOND GINGER

MAKES ½ CUP

2 tbsp almond butter
2 tbsp water
1 tbsp coconut aminos
1 tbsp apple cider vinegar
2 tsp toasted sesame oil
2 drops liquid monk fruit sweetener

juice of ½ lime
1 garlic clove ← *omit for Pitta*
1 tsp freshly grated ginger or ½ tsp ground ginger
⅛ tsp sea salt

In a blender or food processor, combine all ingredients and blend until smooth. Refrigerate in an airtight container for up to 5 days.

SESAME GINGER MISO

1 tbsp freshly grated ginger

1 tbsp white miso

1 tbsp toasted sesame oil

2 tbsp tahini

juice of ½ lime

1 tbsp apple cider or
coconut vinegar

1–2 small garlic cloves, ← *omit for Pitta*
minced

2 tsp coconut aminos or
tamari

1 drop liquid monk fruit or
¼ tsp coconut sugar
(optional)

2 tbsp warm water

In a blender or food processor, combine all ingredients
and blend until smooth. Refrigerate in an airtight
container for up to 5 days.

TURMERIC TAHINI

¼ cup tahini

1 tbsp extra virgin olive oil

juice of ½ lemon

¼ tsp ground turmeric

¼ tsp sea salt

2–6 tbsp hot water

¼ tsp ground cumin
(optional)

¼ tsp ground coriander
(optional)

¼ tsp cayenne pepper (omit
for Pitta)

freshly ground black pepper,
to taste

1 tbsp chopped fresh
parsley

1 In a small bowl, whisk together tahini, olive oil,
lemon juice, turmeric, and salt until well combined.
Add the hot water 1 tbsp at a time, whisking well after
each addition, until the dressing reaches your desired
consistency.

2 Stir in the optional spices, black pepper, and parsley.
Taste and adjust seasoning as desired. Refrigerate in
an airtight container for up to 5 days.

PEANOT SAUCE

¼ cup unsweetened
coconut milk

2 tbsp sunflower seed butter
or almond butter

1 tsp ground ginger

1 drop liquid monk fruit
sweetener or ¼ tsp
coconut sugar

1 tsp apple cider vinegar

juice of ½ lime

2 tsp coconut aminos

¼ tsp turmeric

1 In a small saucepan, combine all ingredients and
bring to a boil. Reduce heat to low and simmer for
5 minutes, stirring frequently, until thickened.

2 Remove from heat and set aside to cool slightly.
Refrigerate in an airtight container for up to 5 days.

*Food is the very first step
on your spiritual path.*

EAT FEEL FRESH
Sauces and Staples

Sauces and extras make a meal. Just because you're eating a plant-based diet doesn't mean you have to give up the flavors of crispy bacon and sour cream. These are my favorite additions to transform a bowl of vegetables into pure magic.

CASHEW SOUR CREAM

MAKES 2 CUPS

1½ cups raw cashews, soaked for 2–4 hours, rinsed, and drained
¾ cup water
2 tsp apple cider vinegar
2 tbsp lemon juice
¼ tsp sea salt
1 tsp nutritional yeast (optional)

In a food processor or high-speed blender, combine all ingredients and blend on high speed for 5–7 minutes until creamy. Scrape down the sides of the blender or add a few drops of water if necessary. Refrigerate in an airtight container for up to 5 days.

HERBAL CASHEW TZATZIKI

MAKES 1 CUP

1 medium cucumber, peeled and grated
1 cup raw cashews, soaked for 2–4 hours, rinsed, and drained
4 tbsp lemon juice
2 tbsp tahini
2 garlic cloves (omit for Pitta)
sea salt and freshly ground black pepper
5–7 tbsp water
⅓ cup chopped fresh dill

1 Place the grated cucumber in a mesh strainer and sprinkle lightly with salt. Set aside to drain for a few minutes while you prepare the cashew paste.

2 In a food processor or high-speed blender, combine cashews, lemon juice, tahini, garlic, and 5 tbsp water. Blend until smooth and creamy, adding more water if needed. Taste and season with salt and pepper.

3 Transfer to a bowl and stir in the grated cucumber and dill. Cover and refrigerate for 2 hours before serving. Tzatziki can be stored in the fridge for up to 4 days.

PLANT-BASED PESTO

2 cups fresh basil leaves, lightly packed

½ cup sunflower seeds or walnuts

½ tsp sea salt

3 garlic cloves, minced ← *omit for Pitta*

1 tbsp lemon juice

¼ cup olive oil, plus more as needed

In a food processor, combine basil, garlic, sunflower seeds, salt, and lemon juice. Pulse while streaming in olive oil until emulsified, stopping to scrape down the bowl once or twice. Refrigerate in an airtight container for 2–3 days.

CHICKPEA MEAT

1 cup cooked chickpeas

½ cup walnuts

1 tbsp coconut aminos, liquid aminos, or gluten-free tamari

In a food processor, combine all ingredients and pulse until the mixture forms coarse crumbles similar to the consistency of cooked ground meat. Refrigerate in an airtight container for up to 5 days.

CHIMICHURRI

½ tbsp dried oregano

2 tbsp hot water

¼ tsp sea salt

1 medium garlic clove (option to omit for Pitta)

1 tbsp apple cider vinegar

zest and juice of ½ lemon

½ cup chopped fresh parsley

½ cup chopped fresh cilantro

¼ serrano pepper, ribs and seeds removed, chopped (option to omit for Pitta)

⅓ tsp crushed red pepper flakes (option to omit for Pitta)

1-2 tbsp olive oil

1 In a small bowl, combine oregano, hot water, and salt and let sit for 5 minutes.

2 Transfer the oregano mixture to a food processor and add all remaining ingredients, except olive oil. Pulse until well combined. With the machine running, stream in the olive oil. Refrigerate in an airtight container for up to 2 days.

COCONUT BACON

1 tbsp coconut aminos or tamari

1 tsp water

½ tsp liquid smoke (optional)

½ tsp monk fruit maple syrup

½ tsp paprika (sweet or smoked)

pinch of sea salt

1 cup large, unsweetened coconut flakes (not shredded)

1 Preheat oven to 350°F. In a medium bowl, whisk together all ingredients except coconut flakes. Add the coconut flakes and toss, stirring until all liquid has been absorbed.

2 Spread the flakes in an even layer on a parchment-lined baking sheet. Cook for 12–14 minutes, stirring every 5 minutes, until coconut is dark in color.

3 Let the "bacon" cool to become crispy then use it immediately or transfer to a freezer-safe bag. Coconut bacon keeps well in the freezer for several months.

Breakfasts
for your Dosha

PARYAVASTHITA (CONTENT)
Chai Pancakes

There's nothing like a stack of healthy pancakes on a self-care Sunday, especially when they cater to your Dosha. These pancakes are warming yet light, and free of wheat, sugar, and eggs. Best paired with a morning Vinyasa flow and a turmeric face mask.

SERVES 4

1 cup quinoa flour
1 cup unsweetened non-dairy milk
1 tbsp sunflower seed butter or almond butter
1 tsp baking powder
1 tsp cinnamon
¼ tsp cardamom
¼ tsp ginger
pinch of ground cloves

can replace with 1 ½ tsp pumpkin pie spice

2 tbsp monk fruit maple syrup or pure maple syrup
1 tsp apple cider vinegar or lemon juice
½ tsp sea salt
coconut oil, for cooking

Vata
Top with almond butter, fresh berries, and monk fruit maple syrup

Pitta
Top with sliced banana, walnuts, and monk fruit maple syrup

Kapha
Top with pomegranate arils and cacao nibs

1 In a large bowl, stir together all ingredients except coconut oil. Let sit for 5 minutes to thicken.

2 In a medium nonstick skillet, heat 1 tsp coconut oil over medium heat. Spoon 2 tbsp of batter into skillet and press into a pancake shape. Cook for 2 minutes, or until the bottom is firm and bubbles begin to appear on the surface.

3 Using a spatula, carefully flip the pancake and cook for 1–2 minutes on the opposite side, taking care not to let it burn. Continue making pancakes until the batter is used up, adding more coconut oil to the pan as needed.

4 Serve warm, topped with the Dosha toppings of your choice.

DIY QUINOA FLOUR

MAKES ⅓ CUP

You can make your own quinoa flour by milling uncooked quinoa in a coffee grinder. Place ¼ cup quinoa in the grinder and pulse on and off, shaking every few pulses to ensure an even grind. This will yield ⅓ cup fine quinoa flour. Refrigerate in an airtight container for up to 6 months.

SURYA (SUN) Smoothies

These satisfying smoothie bowls will brighten even the dreariest morning. Beautiful and balancing, they feature warming spices for Vata, filling coconut butter for Pitta, and light cauliflower for Kapha.

AUTUMN LEAF SMOOTHIE BOWL (Vata)

A warming smoothie bowl with ginger, turmeric, cinnamon, and a root vegetable base is the perfect way to stoke your digestive fire. Vatas are naturally cold, so it's best for them to avoid frozen fruits and favor grounding root veggies instead.

SERVES 1

½ cup cooked butternut squash, pumpkin, or sweet potato

1 tsp cinnamon

¼ tsp ground turmeric

½-in piece fresh ginger, peeled and grated

1 tbsp almond butter

1–2 cups unsweetened non-dairy milk

1 scoop plant-based protein powder (optional)

4 drops liquid monk fruit sweetener or 1 pitted date (optional)

FOR THE SWIRL

⅛ cup cooked butternut squash, pumpkin, or sweet potato

½ tsp spirulina

½ handful of spinach

¼ cup non-dairy milk

TOPPINGS:
pomegranate arils, pumpkin seeds

1 Combine all bowl ingredients in a blender and blend until smooth. Pour into a bowl.

2 Rinse out the blender, then add all swirl ingredients and blend until smooth. Carefully place several small dollops of the swirl mixture on the surface of the smoothie and use a toothpick to create swirls, moving your hand back and forth. Top with pomegranate arils and pumpkin seeds.

Summer Sun Smoothie Bowl (Pitta) — p102

Spring Cheer Smoothie Bowl (Kapha) — p103

SUMMER SUN SMOOTHIE BOWL (Pitta)

If you're a Pitta, you're probably thinking, "A smoothie for breakfast? I'll be hungry in five minutes!" Don't worry; all you need are healthy fats to keep you satiated. Add in some coconut butter or avocado, and watch your Pitta hangry levels disappear.

SERVES 1

½ cup chopped strawberries

1 small banana (for low-glycemic, substitute 1 small zucchini, peeled and diced)

1 cup hibiscus tea, jasmine tea, or coconut milk

2 tbsp chopped fresh cilantro

juice of 1 lime

1 tbsp melted coconut butter or ½ avocado

1 scoop plant-based protein powder (optional)

4 drops liquid monk fruit sweetener or 1 pitted date (optional)

TOPPINGS: sliced strawberries, cilantro, chia seeds

1 Combine all ingredients in a blender and blend until smooth.

2 Pour into a bowl and top with strawberries, chia seeds, and cilantro.

Doshas and Appetite

How do Doshas eat? Let's find out.

VATA   Irregular and unpredictable. Some days they're super hungry and other days they have no appetite. They eat randomly and find it hard to follow a schedule. They prefer snacking to sit-down meals.

PITTA   Regular and ravenous. They need to eat, and on time. If they skip a meal, they become extremely hangry and will become easily irritated with others.

KAPHA   Low appetite, then overeat. Kaphas often eat very little during the day, but then at night, they tend to binge. They may eat for emotional reasons, such as feeling lonely, bored, unfulfilled, or depressed.

SPRING CHEER SMOOTHIE BOWL (Kapha)

I know what you're thinking. Cauliflower in a smoothie? This book just became a little too "fresh" for me. Cauliflower is a creamy, low-glycemic, low-calorie replacement for the usual banana, and with all the other goods in here, you won't taste it at all.

SERVES 1

1 cup blueberries

½ cup steamed cauliflower florets

1–2 cups unsweetened non-dairy milk

1 scoop plant-based protein powder (optional)

½ tsp cinnamon

¼ tsp freshly grated ginger

4 drops liquid monk fruit sweetener or 1 pitted date (optional)

TOPPINGS: blueberries, chia seeds, dragon fruit balls

1 Combine all ingredients in a blender and blend until smooth.

2 Pour into a bowl and top with blueberries, chia seeds, and dragon fruit balls.

LAGHU (EASY)
Lentil Porridge

On one of the first mornings of my Balinese homestay, I was served sweet lentils for breakfast. "Well, this is kinda weird," I thought, "Lentils aren't really a breakfast food." I took a bite and instantly realized how very wrong I was. They're just as easy to make as regular oatmeal, but with more protein and healing benefits.

SERVES 3

1 cup red lentils

2 cups unsweetened coconut milk

1½ cups water

4 drops liquid monk fruit sweetener or
2 tsp coconut sugar

1 tsp cinnamon

pinch of sea salt

Vata
½ cup pumpkin purée

1 tsp pumpkin pie spice

Pitta
1 small apple, chopped

½ tsp alcohol-free vanilla extract

Kapha
1 tsp finely grated ginger

½ tsp ground cardamom

¼ tsp turmeric

⅛ tsp freshly ground black pepper

1 Rinse the lentils well until water runs clear. Place in a bowl, add water to cover, and let soak overnight for optimal digestion.

2 Drain the lentils and place them in a large saucepan. Add coconut milk, water, sweetener, cinnamon, salt, and the ingredients for your Dosha.

3 Bring to a boil over medium-high heat. Once boiling, reduce heat and simmer uncovered for 20 minutes or until most of the liquid is absorbed.

4 Remove from heat and let sit for several minutes to continue to absorb the liquid. Pour into a bowl and enjoy warm.

Multi-cooker: Combine all ingredients and pressure cook on high for 20 minutes. Release pressure manually.

ZAIZAVA (CHILDHOOD)
Sweet Potato Cereal

There are few things as great as milk and cereal. And there are a few things even better—when your milk has no dairy and your cereal has no sugar, wheat, gluten, or chemicals. Yes, we live in a world where all things are possible, and it starts with sweet potato cereal. (Now, if only I could go back in time and swap this for my sugar-Os!)

SERVES 1

1 small sweet potato, diced small

Vata

1–2 cups almond milk
2 tbsp almond butter
2 tbsp chia seeds
pinch of cinnamon

Pitta

1–2 cups coconut milk
2 tbsp coconut flakes
½ cup chopped berries
2 tbsp hemp seeds
pinch of ground cardamom

Kapha

1–2 cups flax milk
½ cup sliced strawberries
2 tbsp pumpkin seeds
pinch of cinnamon
pinch of ground cardamom
pinch of ground ginger

1 Preheat the oven to 400°F. Spread sweet potato chunks in a single layer on a parchment-lined baking sheet. Bake for 20 minutes, until tender and beginning to brown. Let cool to room temperature.

2 Place the cooled sweet potato chunks in a cereal bowl and pour non-dairy milk over top. Add the toppings for your Dosha and eat with a spoon!

ZANTA (SERENE)
Om-meal

The word *om* is the most healing mantra in Sanskrit, comprised of all the primordial sounds of the universe. These om-meal recipes are best paired with a mindful morning for optimal balance.

PUMPKIN PIE OATMEAL (Vata)

Pumpkin helps ground anxious Vatas, who tend to overwhelm themselves by beginning the day without being centered. It contains an amino acid called tryptophan, which is responsible for helping the body make serotonin, the feel-good hormone that makes you calm and relaxed.

—————————— SERVES 1 ——————————

1 cup old-fashioned rolled oats

1¾ cups unsweetened non-dairy milk

¼ cup pumpkin purée

½ tsp ground cinnamon

¼ tsp ground nutmeg

¼ tsp ground cardamom

pinch of ground cloves

can replace with 1 tsp pumpkin pie spice

½ tsp ground vanilla bean

4 drops liquid monk fruit sweetener or
   1 tsp coconut sugar

TOPPINGS: pumpkin seeds, cinnamon, figs

1 In a small saucepan over medium heat, combine oats and milk and bring to a boil. Reduce heat and simmer, stirring occasionally, for 3–5 minutes.

2 Stir in pumpkin purée, cinnamon, nutmeg, cardamom, and cloves and cook until heated through, 1–2 minutes. Add sweetener and stir.

3 Serve warm, drizzled with non-dairy milk and topped with pumpkin seeds, cinnamon, and figs.

Coconut C'oats (Kapha) — p109

Golden Mylk Z'oatmeal (pitta) — p108

Doshas and Dharma

Your Dosha (mind-body constitution) is connected to your Dharma (life-purpose).

VATA — Vatas are meant to work in creative fields. They require a great deal of freedom.

PITTA — Pittas are meant to work in managerial fields. They do best with structure and fast-paced work environments.

KAPHA — Kaphas are meant to work helping people or with their hands. They do best in one-on-one settings and in low-pressure positions.

GOLDEN MYLK Z'OATMEAL (Pitta)

Z'oatmeal swaps zucchini for oats, and delivers tons of detoxifying, cooling, Pitta-balancing benefits. It's light and easy, and best of all, won't leave you craving sugar for the rest of the day. Give it a try—it's pretty z'amazing.

SERVES 1

2 tbsp ground flaxseed
⅓ cup water
¾ cup unsweetened vanilla non-dairy milk
½ cup grated zucchini
½ cup unsweetened applesauce
½ tsp cinnamon
½ tsp turmeric
½ tsp freshly grated ginger
¼ tsp fennel seeds

TOPPINGS: banana, hemp seeds, pomegranate arils

No applesauce on hand? You can replace it with ½ large ripe banana, mashed.

1 In a medium saucepan, make a flax egg by combining ground flaxseed and water. Stir and let sit for 5 minutes to thicken.

2 Add the non-dairy milk to the saucepan with the flax egg and stir to combine. Place over medium-low heat and cook, stirring constantly, for about 2 minutes, until the mixture thickens.

3 Reduce heat to low and stir in the zucchini, applesauce, cinnamon, turmeric, ginger, and fennel seeds.

4 Remove from heat and allow mixture to thicken to desired consistency. Serve warm, topped with sliced banana, hemp seeds, and pomegranate arils.

COCONUT C'OATS (Kapha)

If the name Coconut C'oats doesn't make you want to get all snuggled up with a warm bowl in the morning, I don't what will. However, despite how pajamas-and-chill this name sounds, it's secretly grain-free, though you'd never guess it with such a cozy title. Perfect to get Kaphas, the Hufflepuffs of Ayurveda, on board.

SERVES 1

1 tbsp coconut oil

1 cup raw riced cauliflower (grated cauliflower)

1 tsp cinnamon

½ tsp turmeric

½ cup full-fat coconut milk

1 tbsp ground flaxseed

½ tbsp water

4 drops liquid monk fruit sweetener or 1 tsp coconut sugar

TOPPINGS: unsweetened shredded coconut, slivered almonds, cinnamon

1 In a small saucepan, melt the coconut oil over medium heat. Add the riced cauliflower and cook for about 2 minutes. Sprinkle with cinnamon and turmeric and cook for 1 minute more. Add the coconut milk and simmer for 5 minutes.

2 Meanwhile, make a flax egg by mixing the ground flaxseed and water in a small bowl. Let sit for 5 minutes to thicken.

3 Remove saucepan from heat. Whisk in the flax egg and monk fruit sweetener. Stir continuously until the mixture thickens, about 1 minute.

4 Serve warm, topped with shredded coconut, almonds, and cinnamon.

SUNDARI (SWEET)
Sweet Potato Toast

Move over bread—sweet potatoes are the new plant-based carb of choice! Packed with vitamins and minerals, sweet potato makes the perfect vessel for your favorite sweet and savory toppings. Unlike bread, it keeps blood sugar levels stable so you won't go reaching for another slice. (I mean, maybe you will, but that's just because it tastes so good.)

SERVES 1

1 large sweet potato, scrubbed and ends removed

Vata

SWEET: sliced banana, almond butter, cinnamon, dried goji berries

SAVORY: sliced avocado, tahini, lemon juice, cumin, sea salt, parsley

Pitta

SWEET: coconut yogurt, berries, hemp seeds, almond butter drizzle

SAVORY: **Coconut Bacon** (see p95), mashed black beans, parsley, cilantro

Kapha

SWEET: sunflower seed butter, cinnamon, sliced strawberries, pomegranate arils

SAVORY: hummus, sliced cucumber, lime juice, parsley

1 Preheat the oven to 350°F and line a baking sheet with parchment paper. Cut the sweet potato lengthwise into thin ¼-inch slices.

2 Place the sweet potato slices on the prepared baking sheet. Bake for 15–20 minutes, until they are tender but not cooked all the way through.

3 Remove from the oven and allow to cool completely. Once cool, refrigerate in an airtight container until ready to eat.

4 When ready to serve, pop a slice in the toaster and toast on the highest setting. (It will become warm and bubbly and crispy on the edges.)

5 Add the sweet or savory toppings for your Dosha and enjoy!

SURAMAN (VERY DELIGHTFUL)
Savory Oatmeal

Who says oatmeal has to be sweet? We replace quick oats with steel-cut oatmeal, dried fruit with fibrous vegetables, and sugar with spices to keep you full and satisfied.

WARMING CARROT OATMEAL (Vata)

This oatmeal feels like your favorite soup, with savory thyme, alkalizing spinach, chunks of avocado, and crispy pumpkin seeds. Many Vatas love how grounded they feel after a savory breakfast—give it a try and notice how it affects your energy levels.

SERVES 1

⅔ cup steel-cut oats
2 cups vegetable broth
½ cup shredded carrot
½ tsp dried thyme
1 cup chopped spinach

sea salt and freshly ground black pepper, to taste

TOPPINGS: sliced avocado, pumpkin seeds

1 In a small saucepan, combine the oats, broth, carrot, and thyme. Bring to a boil over medium-high heat, then reduce heat to medium-low and simmer for 20 minutes. Stir in chopped spinach and cook for 3 minutes more until spinach is wilted and oats are fully cooked.

2 Remove from heat and drain any remaining liquid. Season with salt and pepper to taste, and serve topped with avocado and pumpkin seeds.

Turmeric Chickpea Oatmeal (Kapha)—p.115

Lentil Squash Oatmeal (Pitta)—p.114

LENTIL SQUASH OATMEAL (Pitta)

Pittas need a hearty breakfast, otherwise they'll get seriously hangry. Energizing steel-cut oats and butternut squash, protein-rich lentils, and healthy-fat coconut milk and avocado keep a Pitta's mood, mind, and muscles feelin' right.

SERVES 1

¼ cup cooked red lentils

⅓ cup steel-cut oats

1½ cups coconut milk

¼ cup cubed and roasted butternut squash

1 tsp curry powder or ½ tsp dried thyme

pinch of sea salt

TOPPINGS: sliced avocado, cucumber, hemp seeds

1 In a saucepan, combine lentils, oats, coconut milk, squash, curry powder or thyme, and salt. Bring to a boil over medium-high heat. Once boiling, reduce heat to medium-low and simmer for 20–25 minutes until oats are fully cooked.

2 Remove from heat and let sit for 5 minutes to thicken and cool down to a palatable temperature. Serve topped with sliced avocado, cucumber, and hemp seeds.

Doshas and Dreams

Did you know the dreams you have are connected to your Dosha?

VATA DREAMS	Fleeing, flying, floating, falling, fulfillment, autumn. Generally very active.
PITTA DREAMS	Problem-solving, real-life situations, arriving somewhere too late, summer. Generally very realistic.
KAPHA DREAMS	No dreams or very faded memory. Finding money, eating sweets, sex, snow, spring. Generally very sweet.

TURMERIC CHICKPEA OATMEAL (Kapha)

Steel-cut oats and chickpeas deliver the fiber and protein Kaphas need for long-lasting fullness. Toss in some fat-burning spices, load in the fibrous greens, and you have a warming yet detoxifying breakfast that's reminiscent of mac n' cheese.

SERVES 1

½ cup steel-cut oats

⅓ cup cooked chickpeas

½ cup water

½ cup unsweetened non-dairy milk

1 tbsp nutritional yeast

½ tsp turmeric

2 tsp freshly grated ginger or
   ½ tsp ground ginger

pinch of sea salt and freshly ground
   black pepper

1 cup baby spinach

TOPPINGS: tahini, parsley, roasted
   chickpeas

1 In a saucepan, combine oats, chickpeas, water, non-dairy milk, nutritional yeast, turmeric, ginger, salt, and pepper. Bring to a boil over medium-high heat. Once boiling, reduce heat to medium-low, add spinach, and simmer for 20–25 minutes.

2 Once creamy, remove from heat and let sit for 5 minutes to thicken and cool down to a palatable temperature. Serve topped with a drizzle of tahini and a sprinkling of parsley and chia seeds.

CHANDRA (MOON)
Chia Pudding

Make this "moon" pudding at night, and the next morning you'll wake up to a creamy, indulgent breakfast. Chia seeds are rich in omega-3s and a must for anyone on a plant-based diet. The overnight soak transforms them into a decadent pudding.

SERVES 1

1 cup unsweetened non-dairy milk
3 tbsp chia seeds

Vata
¼ tsp ground cinnamon
⅛–¼ tsp ground ginger
pinch of ground cloves
¼ tsp alcohol-free vanilla extract
1 drop liquid monk fruit sweetener

TOPPINGS: sliced banana, raw honey, chopped pistachios

Pitta
¼ tsp alcohol-free vanilla extract
2 tbsp unsweetened coconut flakes
4 drops liquid monk fruit sweetener

TOPPINGS: diced mango, coconut flakes

Kapha
¼ tsp alcohol-free vanilla extract
½ cup raspberries
1 tbsp lemon juice
1 tbsp lemon zest
⅛ tsp ground cardamom
4 drops liquid monk fruit sweetener

TOPPINGS: raspberries, lemon zest

1 In a small bowl, combine non-dairy milk, chia seeds, and the ingredients for your Dosha (except toppings).

2 Cover and refrigerate for at least 30 minutes or overnight. (The chia seeds will become more gelatinous the longer they soak.)

3 Before serving, stir well. Add the toppings for your Dosha and enjoy!

Make a big batch and separate into several small containers to enjoy for a quick breakfast or snack. It keeps covered in the fridge for 5 days.

SHANTI (PEACEFUL)
Quinoa Porridge

Quinoa porridge is the perfect contemporary Ayurvedic breakfast—
easy on the digestive system and even easier to make. It's customized
for your Dosha with more warming spices for Vata, cooling berries
and mint for Pitta, and stimulating qualities for Kapha.

SERVES 1

½ cup cooked quinoa

1 cup unsweetened vanilla
non-dairy milk

Vata

½ chopped organic apple

1 tsp cinnamon

¼ tsp freshly grated ginger

¼ tsp ground cardamom

4 drops liquid monk fruit
sweetener

pinch of sea salt

TOPPINGS: almond butter,
cinnamon, chia seeds

Pitta

½ cup sliced strawberries

2 tbsp hemp seeds

½ tsp cinnamon

4 drops liquid monk fruit
sweetener

TOPPINGS: mint leaves, fresh
berries, hemp seeds

Kapha

1 tsp cinnamon

½ tsp ground ginger

1 tsp ground cardamom

1 tsp ground cloves

½ tsp freshly ground white or
black pepper

pinch of sea salt

2 tbsp flax seeds

2 tbsp organic instant coffee or
1 shot espresso (optional)

4 drops liquid monk fruit
sweetener

TOPPINGS: cinnamon, flax seeds,
cacao nibs, grated ginger

1 In a small saucepan, combine
cooked quinoa, non-dairy milk, and
the ingredients for your Dosha (except
toppings). Bring to a simmer and cook,
covered, for about 10 minutes.

2 Remove from heat and serve with
the toppings for your Dosha.

This porridge reheats
well, so make it
the night before for
an easy morning!

CHINMAYA (FULL OF CONSCIOUSNESS)
Chickpea Flour Frittatas

Just because you're plant-based doesn't mean you can't enjoy frittatas. They're back on the menu with a sneaky little ingredient: chickpeas. Yes, these creamy beans can take the place of eggs. Give this a shot with your family and see if they can tell the difference.

SERVES 2

1¾ cups water
1¼ cups chickpea flour
¼ tsp turmeric
1 tsp sea salt
sliced avocado, to serve
chopped fresh parsley, to garnish

Vata

1 tbsp sesame oil
1 cup peeled and diced sweet potato
1 cup baby spinach
1 garlic clove, minced
1 medium yellow onion, diced

Pitta

1 tbsp coconut oil
2 medium zucchinis, thinly sliced
2 tbsp tahini
2 tbsp nutritional yeast
1 tsp curry powder

Kapha

1 tbsp grapeseed oil
2 cups finely chopped kale
2 cups sliced mushrooms
1 medium yellow onion, diced

1 Preheat oven to 400°F. In a medium bowl, whisk together the water, chickpea flour, turmeric, and salt. Allow the mixture to set for 5 minutes while preparing the vegetables.

2 In a medium cast iron skillet, heat the oil for your Dosha over medium heat. Add the vegetables and seasonings for your Dosha and sauté until soft or wilted.

3 Pour the chickpea flour batter into the skillet and cook for 5 minutes, until edges begin to brown. Transfer the skillet to the preheated oven and bake for 35 minutes.

If you don't have a cast iron skillet, transfer the mixture to an oiled baking dish before placing in the oven.

4 Remove from oven and allow to cool for at least 10 minutes. (This is crucial for the consistency; otherwise it will be too mushy and fall apart.) Serve warm, room temperature, or cold. Top with sliced avocado and parsley.

GANAPATI (CONSCIOUSNESS)
Grain-Free N'oatmeal

The mantra *Om Ganapati Om* is used to remove all obstacles—such as not knowing what to eat for breakfast. It's one of the best mantras to start your day for smooth sailing and to help you become your highest self.

Spiced Peach & Squash N'oatmeal (pitta) — p122

Strawberry Shortcake N'oatmeal (kapha) — p123

SWEET POTATO GINGER N'OATMEAL (Vata)

If you have a baked sweet potato, you can throw this together in three minutes flat. Ginger and cinnamon will warm you from within, while coconut butter gives you healthy fat to fuel your body for the day—exactly what a cold Vata needs.

SERVES 1

1 cup mashed sweet potato
½ cup unsweetened non-dairy milk
1 tbsp freshly grated ginger
1 tsp cinnamon
1 tbsp coconut butter, melted
4 drops liquid monk fruit sweetener or
   1 tsp coconut sugar
pinch of pink Himalayan salt
   1 scoop plant-based protein powder (optional)

TOPPINGS: almond butter, cinnamon, pumpkin seeds, flax seeds

1 In a small saucepan, combine all ingredients and warm over medium heat for 2–3 minutes.

2 Transfer to a bowl and top with a swirl of almond butter, pumpkin seeds, flax seeds, and cinnamon.

SPICED PEACH & SQUASH N'OATMEAL (Pitta)

This light but nourishing breakfast is just what a hungry Pitta needs. Spaghetti squash provides fuel, and cooling coconut and peach pair well with digestive-enhancing ginger. Plant protein and hemp seeds are satiating for a productive Pitta day.

SERVES 1

1½ cups cooked spaghetti squash

1 cup unsweetened coconut milk

1 large ripe peach, diced or 8 frozen peach slices, thawed and diced

½ tbsp freshly grated ginger or 1 tsp ground ginger

1 tsp cinnamon

pinch of pink Himalayan salt

4 drops liquid monk fruit sweetener or 1 tsp coconut sugar

1 scoop plant-based protein powder (optional)

TOPPINGS: hemp seeds, toasted coconut, grilled peaches

1 In a large saucepan, stir together all ingredients except for the optional protein powder and bring to a boil over high heat. Reduce to a simmer and cook for 6–8 minutes, stirring frequently, and pulling apart the fibers of the squash.

2 Stir in protein powder, if using, and remove from heat. Let cool for a few minutes before serving. Serve topped with hemp seeds, toasted coconut, and grilled peaches, if desired.

The n'oatmeal may look dry at the beginning. However, the peaches emit liquid as they cook, which will amp up the liquid. If it's still dry at the end, add some milk.

122

Balancing Affirmations

VATA	I deserve the time to sit down and enjoy a meal.
	I feel whole with every meal.
PITTA	Food is not going anywhere. I enjoy my food in peace.
	Mealtimes are a welcome break in my day.
KAPHA	I eat when I am hungry, I stop when I am full.
	Food is my nourishment, I am already whole.
	I release past guilt and shame around eating.

STRAWBERRY SHORTCAKE N'OATMEAL (Kapha)

You read that correctly, sweet Kapha—strawberry shortcake is what we're cookin' for breakfast! Except this shortcake has a covert little companion—cauliflower. Yes, this mild and creamy vegetable is back to make your shortcake dreams come true.

SERVES 1

1 cup non-dairy milk

¼ cup raw riced cauliflower (grated cauliflower)

¼ cup unsweetened shredded coconut

1 cup chopped strawberries

2 tbsp ground flaxseed or chia seeds

½ tsp alcohol-free vanilla extract

½ tsp cinnamon

4 drops liquid monk fruit sweetener or 1 tsp coconut sugar

TOPPINGS: sliced strawberries, cinnamon, chia seeds

1 In a small saucepan, combine all ingredients and heat over medium heat until just beginning to bubble. Simmer for 1–2 minutes, stirring gently.

2 Remove from the heat and let cool for a few minutes before serving. Serve topped with sliced strawberries, cinnamon, and chia seeds.

Six-Taste Bowls

BUILDING A
Six-Taste Bowl

Six-Taste Bowls fulfill the six tastes of Ayurveda and leave you nourished on a cellular level. Keep precooked grains, legumes, and sweet potatoes on hand and you're only minutes away from a healthy, satisfying lunch.

SOUR
Squeeze a lemon or lime over your bowl to fulfill the sour taste.

SWEET
Healthy fats, like avocado, and hearty root veggies, like sweet potato, bring sweetness to your bowls.

SIX-TASTE BOWL COMPONENTS

The Six-Taste Bowl recipes in this chapter include the same basic components to build in all six tastes: salty, sweet, sour, bitter, pungent, and astringent. Mix and match ingredients to create your own bowls!

HEARTY BASE (SWEET)
Healthy grains: quinoa, barley, brown rice

Starchy vegetables: sweet potato, pumpkin, butternut squash, carrot, beet

HEALTHY FATS (SWEET)
Avocado, coconut, nut cheeses, almonds, cashews

Plant-based oils: olive, sesame, coconut, avocado, grapeseed

COLORFUL VEGGIES (BITTER)
Leafy greens: spinach, arugula, collard, kale

Cruciferous vegetables: cauliflower, broccoli, cabbage, brussels sprouts

Zucchini, snow peas, bell pepper, cucumber

SPICES & AROMATICS (PUNGENT)
Cumin, turmeric, ginger, asafetida, black pepper

Allium vegetables: garlic, onion, leek, scallion, shallot

PLANT PROTEIN (ASTRINGENT)
Legumes: lentils, black beans, chickpeas, adzuki beans, edamame

Nuts and seeds: almonds, sunflower seeds, chia seeds, flax seeds, walnuts, tahini

GARNISHES (SALTY, SOUR, ASTRINGENT)
Sea salt, coconut aminos, sea vegetables, celery

Lemon, lime, apple cider or coconut vinegar

Cilantro, dill, sprouts, microgreens, sesame seeds, chia seeds

BITTER
Fill your bowl with broccoli and leafy greens for bitterness.

FEED YOUR DOSHA

You can customize any bowl for your Dosha by including more of the tastes that pacify it and less of the tastes that increase it— just make sure all six tastes are still present in your bowl.

Vata

Include more sweet, sour, and salty tastes. Decrease bitter, pungent, and astringent tastes.

Pitta

Include more sweet, bitter, and astringent tastes. Decrease sour, salty, and pungent tastes.

Kapha

Include more bitter, pungent, and astringent tastes. Decrease sweet, sour, and salty tastes.

ASTRINGENT
A sprinkle of sunflower seeds and a handful of sprouts add astringency.

PUNGENT
Roast vegetables with spices like turmeric, ginger, and cumin for pungency.

SALTY
A few strips of seaweed are a great way to build in saltiness.

ASVADYA (DELICIOUS)
Thai Buddha Bowl

I used to throw peanut butter in everything—my sauces, my smoothies, my mouth. Then I learned peanuts are not actually nuts, but super acidic legumes susceptible to a carcinogenic mold called aflatoxin, which also feeds candida. Not so appetizing. I switched to sunflower seed butter and my life (and pH levels) have never been better! I kid you pea*not*!

SERVES 1

1 cup cooked quinoa
½ cup bean sprouts
½ cup snow peas
½ cup shredded carrots
½ cup shredded purple cabbage ← *option to steam for vata & kapha*
2–4 tbsp **Peanot Sauce** (see p93)

TOPPINGS: sunflower seeds, fresh cilantro, sliced scallions, lime wedges

1 Spread quinoa in a wide bowl and add bean sprouts, snow peas, carrots, and cabbage.

2 Drizzle with warm Peanot Sauce and top with sunflower seeds, cilantro, scallions, and a squeeze of lime.

Six Tastes

SWEET	SOUR	SALTY	BITTER	PUNGENT	ASTRINGENT
quinoa, carrot, sunflower seed butter (sauce)	lime, vinegar (sauce)	coconut aminos (sauce)	snow peas, cilantro, purple cabbage	scallion, ginger (sauce), turmeric (sauce)	sprouts, turmeric (sauce)

VISAPAGAMA (DETOXIFYING)
Chipotle Bowl

Did you just read the words "detoxifying" and "chipotle" in the same title? (And not, "I need to detox because I ate too much Chipotle.") Yep, life just got real good. In Ayurveda, spices are considered the most detoxifying foods out there because they rev up your metabolism, allowing your body to move toxins through the system.

SERVES 1

reduce or omit for Pitta →
1 tbsp avocado or grapeseed oil
→ 2 garlic cloves, minced

replace with 1 fennel bulb for Pitta →
1 small white onion, diced

replace with 1 cup chopped broccoli for Pitta →
1 red bell pepper, sliced

option to omit for Pitta →
½ tsp chipotle chile powder
½ tsp sea salt
1 cup **Cilantro Lime Cauliflower Rice** (see p192)
½ cup cubed and roasted butternut squash with 1 tsp paprika

¼ cup **Low FODMAP Salsa** (see p198)
½ cup **Mexican Chipotle Roasted Chickpeas** (see p196)
½ avocado, sliced

TOPPINGS: shredded lettuce, fresh cilantro, lime wedges ← *option to omit for Vata*

1 In a large skillet, heat oil over medium-high heat. Add the garlic, onion, pepper, chipotle powder, and salt. Sauté for 5–7 minutes or until vegetables are soft. Remove from heat.

2 Spread the rice in a bowl and add the sautéed veggies, roasted squash, salsa, chipotle chickpeas, and avocado. Top with lettuce, cilantro, and a squeeze of lime.

Six Tastes

SWEET	SOUR	SALTY	BITTER	PUNGENT	ASTRINGENT
butternut squash, avocado	lime	sea salt	cilantro, cauliflower	red bell pepper, chipotle, garlic, onion	chickpeas

NAVINA (FRESH)
Chimichurri Cauliflower Rice Bowl

Chimichurri, a light Argentinian herb-based sauce, is a refreshing mixture of parsley, cilantro, oregano, and olive oil. It's like a Latin American pesto, minus the cheese, plus a kiss of red pepper. It brings vibrant flavor and color to cauliflower rice.

SERVES 2

1 tbsp olive oil

option to omit for Pitta → 2 garlic cloves, minced

3–4 cups raw riced cauliflower (from 1 head of cauliflower)

½ tsp sea salt

½ cup **Chimichurri** (see p95)

1 cup cubed and roasted butternut squash

1 cup cooked adzuki beans

TOPPINGS: fresh cilantro, pomegranate arils, lemon wedges

1 In large skillet, heat the oil over medium high heat. Add the garlic and cook for 30 seconds. Add the riced cauliflower and salt and cook for 5–7 minutes, stirring frequently, until the cauliflower is slightly crispy on the outside and tender on the inside. Remove from heat and mix in the chimichurri sauce.

2 To assemble, spread 1 cup chimichurri rice in a wide bowl and top with ½ cup roasted squash and ½ cup adzuki beans. Garnish with fresh cilantro, pomegranate, and a squeeze of lemon.

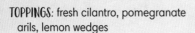

Six Tastes

SWEET	SOUR	SALTY	BITTER	PUNGENT	ASTRINGENT
butternut squash, pomegranate	lemon, vinegar (sauce)	sea salt	cilantro, olive oil, cauliflower	garlic	adzuki beans

PRACINA (CLASSIC)
Deconstructed Bruschetta Bowl

Want to know the number one thing I craved while I was living in India? Simple food. Don't get me wrong, I love my spices, but sometimes a girl just wants some plain old veggies without curry sauce. Italian cuisine puts the veggies center stage, with simple seasonings that allow the flavors of the vegetables to come through.

SERVES 2

steamed for Vata & Kapha →

replace with steamed broccoli for Pitta →

option to omit for Pitta →

- 1 cup cooked barley
- 2 cups baby spinach
- ¼ cup roasted red pepper
- 1 small zucchini, sliced
- 1 cup canned artichoke hearts, sliced
- 8 cherry tomatoes
- 4 pitted green olives

- 4 tbsp **Plant-Based Goat Cheese** (see p135)
- 2 tbsp **Plant-Based Pesto** (see p95)
- 2 tbsp **Italian Dressing** (see p92)

TOPPINGS: fresh basil, sliced almonds

1 Spread barley in a wide bowl and top with spinach, peppers, zucchini, artichoke hearts, tomatoes, olives, plant-based goat cheese, and pesto.

2 Drizzle dressing over top and top with fresh basil and sliced almonds.

Six Tastes

SWEET	SOUR	SALTY	BITTER	PUNGENT	ASTRINGENT
barley, plant-based goat cheese, almonds	tomato, lemon (dressing), vinegar (dressing)	sea salt (dressing)	basil, spinach, zucchini, olives, pesto	roasted pepper, black pepper	artichoke

PLANT-BASED GOAT CHEESE

The first time I tasted nut-based cheese at a raw-vegan restaurant in NYC, I was floored. How was it not front-page news that you could make cheese out of nuts? I ended up going to plant-based culinary school to learn the craft of raw-vegan cheese. This is my go-to for a delicious cheese that requires no fermentation or hesitation.

MAKES 4 OZ

1 cup raw cashews, soaked overnight and drained

juice of 1 lemon

½ cup water

1 tbsp olive oil

¼ tsp sea salt

¼ cup chopped fresh herbs, such as dill or parsley, for coating (optional)

1 In a food processor, combine all ingredients except herbs. Blend until smooth and creamy, scraping down the bowl as needed.

2 Place two layers of cheesecloth over a mesh strainer and scoop mixture onto the cheesecloth. Gather corners at top and twist to form a disc. Secure with tape or rubber band. (No need to squeeze.)

3 Set the strainer on a bowl and refrigerate for 12 hours or overnight, until it holds form within the cheese cloth.

4 If desired, coat with fresh herbs. Place herbs on wax paper and roll the cheese over the mixture, coating the sides. Press somewhat firmly, so the herbs stick to the outside of the cheese.

5 Place in an airtight container or wrap tightly in plastic wrap and refrigerate until ready to use. Cheese can be stored for up to 5 days.

DURGA (WARRIOR GODDESS)
Goddess Bowl

Durga is the fierce warrior goddess whose name means "the invincible one." After eating this bowl, you may start channeling her. Protein-packed quinoa, hemp seeds, and hummus are balanced by cooling spinach, cucumber, and parsley. Add the endurance-building healthy fats from avocado, cashews, and tahini, and you've got yourself ready for battle.

SERVES 1

steamed for vata & kapha →

½ cup cooked quinoa
2 cups baby spinach
4 baby beets, steamed and sliced

Option to omit for Pitta →

4 cherry tomatoes, sliced
½ cup sliced cucumber
½ avocado, thinly sliced

2 tbsp **Edamame Hummus** (see p201)
  or **Chickpea Meat** (see p95)
2 tbsp finely chopped parsley
1 tbsp hemp seeds
2 tbsp **Herbal Cashew Tzatziki** (see p94)

1 Spread quinoa in a wide bowl and top with spinach, beets, tomatoes, cucumber, avocado, and hummus or chickpea meat.

2 Sprinkle with parsley and hemp seeds and serve with tzatziki sauce.

Six Tastes

SWEET	SOUR	SALTY	BITTER	PUNGENT	ASTRINGENT
beets, quinoa, avocado	lemon (tzatziki), tomato	sea salt	parsley, spinach, cucumber, dill (tzatziki)	garlic	tahini, edamame (hummus), hemp seeds

DIPIKA (LIGHT)
Lebanese Lentil Bowl

I love Lebanese food—it's light, versatile, and perfect for when you want a little bit of variety on your plate. This bowl is no different. Protein-rich lentils pair beautifully with grounding butternut squash and pungent spices, which are brightened up with refreshing herbs and a bite of salty almond feta. The only thing that's missing is an Arabic dance party at the end.

SERVES 1

1 tbsp olive oil

omit for Pitta → 1 garlic clove, very finely minced

½ cup cooked green or brown lentils

½ cup cubed and roasted butternut squash

1 baby eggplant, cubed and roasted

2 tbsp **Mediterranean Dressing** (see p92)

2 tbsp **Almond Feta** (see p139)

TOPPINGS: lemon juice, dill, mint, parsley

1 In a medium skillet, heat 1 tbsp olive oil over medium heat. Reduce heat to low, add garlic, and cook for 1–2 minutes until fragrant but not brown.

2 Add the lentils, squash, eggplant, and dressing to the pan. Increase heat to medium and cook for 1–2 minutes, stirring gently, until ingredients are warm and well combined.

3 To serve, transfer to a bowl then top with almond feta. Squeeze lemon juice over top and sprinkle with dill, parsley, and mint. Serve warm for Vata and Kapha; for Pitta serve warm or cold.

Six Tastes

SWEET	SOUR	SALTY	BITTER	PUNGENT	ASTRINGENT
butternut squash, almond feta	lemon	sea salt (dressing)	parsley, dill	garlic, cumin (dressing)	lentils

ALMOND FETA

When I was in middle school, I ate a Greek salad almost every day, because, well, feta. I didn't realize that a plate of iceberg lettuce with a mountain of feta wasn't exactly nutrient-dense. Whoops. Over a dairy-free decade later, I still missed the tangy saltiness that only feta could deliver, so I created a plant-based version to satisfy my feta-tooth—without involving a cow.

SERVES 4

1 cup raw almonds (soaked overnight and skins removed) or blanched almonds (soaked overnight)

⅓ cup lemon juice

3 tbsp extra virgin olive oil

omit for Pitta → 1 garlic clove, peeled

1½ tsp sea salt

½ cup water

2 tsp fresh or dried herbs such as rosemary, thyme, and oregano, plus more for coating (optional)

For a completely raw version, use a dehydrator to dry cheese for 4–6 hours instead of baking in the oven.

1 Drain and rinse the soaked almonds. In a food processor or high-speed blender, combine almonds, lemon juice, olive oil, garlic, salt, and water. Blend for 3–6 minutes until very creamy. Stir in herbs, if using.

2 Scoop the mixture into a nut milk bag or triple-layered cheesecloth and squeeze out the excess liquid. Place in a strainer over a bowl and tie the loose ends of the cheese cloth to create a ball. *← Use it as a cheese spread as is, or follow the next step for the full feta experience.* Refrigerate for several hours or overnight.

3 Preheat oven to 225°F and line a baking sheet with parchment paper. Remove cheese from cloth and shape into a square about ¾ inch thick. Bake for 40 minutes until the top is slightly firm. Let cool, then refrigerate.

4 Once cold, coat with fresh or dried herbs, if desired. Store in airtight container in refrigerator for up to 2 days.

PAURASTYA (EASTERN)
Sesame Ginger Miso Bowl

When I see the words sesame, ginger, or miso on a menu, I immediately know exactly what I'm going to order. When all three are paired together, I know I'm in for a real treat. This recipe is my ideal on-the-go meal because it tastes great at room temperature and it's super easy to pack in a Mason jar for travel.

SERVES 1

½ cup cooked quinoa or brown rice

½ cup cooked edamame

option to omit for vata → 2 cups arugula or baby spinach

1 nori sheet, cut into eight pieces

½ cup grated carrot

½ avocado, sliced

½ English cucumber, thinly sliced

2 tbsp alfalfa sprouts

2 tbsp **Sesame Ginger Miso Dressing** (see p93)

TOPPINGS: black sesame or hemp seeds, fresh mint, sliced scallions

1 Place quinoa in a bowl and add arugula, carrot, edamame, avocado, cucumber, nori, and sprouts.

2 Drizzle with dressing and top with sesame or hemp seeds, fresh mint, and sliced scallions

Six Tastes

SWEET	SOUR	SALTY	BITTER	PUNGENT	ASTRINGENT
quinoa or rice, carrots, avocado	lime (dressing)	nori, miso (dressing)	scallions, arugula, spinach, cucumber	garlic (dressing), ginger (dressing)	sesame seeds, edamame, sprouts

VIVIKTA (NEAT)
Bento Box Sushi Bowl

Bento boxes have to be one of the cutest inventions of all time. They're organized, compact, and ensure all your ingredients don't get all mixed together when you toss it in your bag. This deconstructed bowl will satisfy your sushi craving, and it's a great way to sneak more bitter tastes into your diet without even realizing it.

SERVES 1

½ cup cooked cauliflower rice or
  brown rice
1 serving **Carrot Slaw**
1 serving **Seaweed Salad**
2 tbsp **Edamame Hummus** (see p201)
½ avocado, sliced

steamed for Vata & Kapha → ¼ cup sliced purple cabbage

2 tbsp **Almond Ginger Dressing**
  (see p92)
black and white sesame seeds, to garnish

1 Place rice in a bento box or bowl and top with edamame hummus. Add a scoop of carrot slaw and a scoop of seaweed salad.

2 Top with sliced avocado and red cabbage. Drizzle with dressing, and garnish with sesame seeds.

Six Tastes

SWEET	SOUR	SALTY	BITTER	PUNGENT	ASTRINGENT
avocado, carrot, almonds (dressing)	lime (slaw), vinegar (seaweed salad)	sea salt (dressing), coconut aminos (dressing), seaweed	cauliflower, cucumber, cabbage, seaweed	radish, ginger (dressing)	edamame (hummus), sesame seeds

CARROT SLAW

SERVES 2

2 medium carrots, shredded
3 large radishes, shredded
¼ tsp lime zest
1 tbsp lime juice
1 tbsp olive oil
2 tbsp **Almond Ginger Dressing** (see p92)

In a medium bowl, toss together all ingredients. Refrigerate for at least 10 minutes before serving.

SEAWEED SALAD

SERVES 2

2oz dried kombu
2 garlic cloves, crushed (option to omit for Pitta)
1 tbsp apple cider vinegar
1 tbsp sesame oil
1 tbsp coconut aminos
sea salt, to taste

Bring a small pot of water to boil and add the kombu. Simmer for 30 minutes, until tender, then cool before cutting into thin strips. Place in a bowl and add remaining ingredients. Mix well and refrigerate for at least 10 minutes before serving.

ZUDDHA (PURE)
Quinoa Sunflower Seed Pesto Bowl

You know when you eat a meal and just want to do a happy dance because you feel so light, bright, and energized? That's how this bowl will make you feel. Springy pesto will have you feeling like a sunflower, with petals of zucchini and blossoms of acorn squash. What a way to sneak in bitter tastes while still being so sweet!

SERVES 1

2 medium zucchinis

1 cup cooked quinoa

¼ acorn squash, roasted and sliced

½ cup **Mediterranean Herb Roasted Chickpeas** (see p196)

2 tbsp **Plant-Based Pesto** (see p95), divided

TOPPINGS: microgreens, sunflower seeds or walnuts

1 Using the straight blade of a spiralizer, slice the zucchinis into thin ribbons. Bring a small pot of water to boil and add the zucchini. Cook for 2 minutes, then strain immediately and let it drain for 3 minutes.

2 To assemble, place the quinoa in a large bowl and stir in 1 tbsp pesto. Top with roasted acorn squash, zucchini ribbons, roasted chickpeas, and remaining 1 tbsp pesto. Garnish with microgreens and sunflower seeds.

Six Tastes

SWEET	SOUR	SALTY	BITTER	PUNGENT	ASTRINGENT
acorn squash, quinoa	lemon (pesto)	sea salt (pesto, chickpeas)	zucchini, microgreens, olive oil (pesto), basil (pesto)	garlic (pesto)	chickpeas, sunflower seeds or walnuts

AGADA (HEALTHY)
Rainbow Pad Thai Bowl

Eating the rainbow has never been easier or more delicious with this "pad thai" bowl. With a few swirls of a spiralizer, you create vegetable "noodles," which pair beautifully with a tangy and nutty almond-ginger dressing. You can choose to enjoy it raw, or cook it for a warming, nourishing meal.

SERVES 1

4oz kelp noodles
½ cup spiralized zucchini
½ cup spiralized beets
½ cup spiralized carrots
¼ cup cooked edamame
2–4 tbsp **Almond Ginger Dressing** (see p92)
½ tbsp coconut oil (if cooking)

TOPPINGS: slivered almonds, fresh cilantro, sprouts, black sesame seeds, lime wedges

Drain and rinse kelp noodles. Place them in a bowl of warm water and let soak for about 10 minutes while you prepare the other ingredients. (This helps to soften and separate them.)

Raw version (best for Pitta): Toss spiralized vegetables and kelp noodles in a serving bowl. Add edamame and drizzle with dressing. Top with slivered almonds, cilantro, sprouts, black sesame seeds, and a squeeze of lime.

Cooked version (best for Vata/Kapha): In a medium skillet, heat coconut oil over medium heat. Add spiralized vegetables and kelp noodles. Add 4 tbsp dressing and cook for 3–5 minutes, stirring gently, until warm and thoroughly coated. Serve topped with edamame, slivered almonds, cilantro, sprouts, black sesame seeds, and a squeeze of lime.

Six Tastes

SWEET	SOUR	SALTY	BITTER	PUNGENT	ASTRINGENT
carrot, beet, almonds, almond butter (dressing)	lime	kelp noodles, sea salt (dressing)	kelp noodles, cilantro, zucchini	ginger (dressing)	edamame, sprouts, black sesame seeds

MIZRA (MIXED)
Fajita Bowl

Nothing says "party" quite like fajitas, am I right? The celebration of vegetables dancing in a simmering bowl of spices really gets you in a festive mood, probably because it's so *rajasic* in nature, with pungent onion, garlic, and peppers. Cooling herbs and spices such as coriander, fennel, and cilantro balance this heating dish, so you can keep your fire to the dance floor (and not the digestion).

SERVES 2

1 tbsp grapeseed or avocado oil

2 garlic cloves, minced (replace with ¼ tsp asafetida for Pitta)

1 red onion, sliced (replace with 1 fennel bulb for Pitta)

2 large red bell peppers, sliced *(replace with 1 cup chopped broccoli for Pitta)*

1 cup baby bella mushrooms, sliced

4 cups baby spinach

½ tsp ground cumin

½ tsp ground coriander

½ tsp ground fennel

½ tsp chili powder *(omit for Pitta)*

½ tsp Hungarian or smoked paprika

½ tsp sea salt

juice of ½ lime

1 cup **Cilantro Lime Rice** (see p195)

½ cup **Cumin Guacamole** (see p198)

¼ cup **Cashew Sour Cream** (see p94)

fresh cilantro, to garnish

1 In a large skillet, heat the oil over medium-high heat. Add the garlic, onion, and bell peppers, and sauté for about 5 minutes until soft.

2 Reduce heat to medium and add the mushrooms, spinach, cumin, coriander, fennel, chili powder, paprika, and salt. Sauté for 3–5 minutes until mushrooms are soft and the spinach is wilted.

3 To assemble, spread rice in a wide bowl and top with sautéed vegetables and a squeeze of lime. Serve with guacamole and cashew sour cream. Garnish with cilantro.

Six Tastes

SWEET	SOUR	SALTY	BITTER	PUNGENT	ASTRINGENT
rice, cashews (sour cream), avocado, (guacamole)	lime	sea salt	cilantro, spinach	garlic, onion, chili powder, cumin, coriander, paprika	mushroom

SVATTA (SPICED)
Turmeric Tahini Bowl

I sneak in turmeric and tahini anywhere I can. Turmeric because it's a natural mood-enhancer, fat-burner, and inflammation-zapper. Tahini because it's nutty and delivers that satiating, healthy-fat taste I love. Together, these two can make anything magical, especially this bowl with quinoa, lentils, sweet potato, and kale. So much yes.

SERVES 1

½ cup cooked quinoa

½ cup cooked brown lentils

1 medium sweet potato, diced and roasted

1 cup steamed or sautéed kale

½ avocado, sliced

2 tbsp **Turmeric Tahini Dressing** (see p93)

2 tbsp wild nori flakes, to garnish

1 watermelon radish, sliced, to garnish

1 Spread quinoa in a wide bowl and add lentils, sweet potato, kale, and avocado.

2 Drizzle with dressing and garnish with nori flakes and sliced watermelon radish.

Six Tastes

SWEET	SOUR	SALTY	BITTER	PUNGENT	ASTRINGENT
quinoa, avocado, sweet potato	lemon (dressing)	nori flakes	kale, nori flakes	radish, turmeric (dressing)	lentils, tahini (dressing), turmeric (dressing)

JANAPADA (COUNTRY)
Southwestern Quinoa Salad Bowl

The Southwest just became Ayurvedic with this sattvic dish. Cumin is a tridoshic spice that enhances digestion, improves nutrient absorption, and helps flush out toxins. It can even reduce gas caused by beans—which may be why it's a staple in every legume-rich cuisine.

SERVES 1

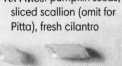
replace with steamed baby beets for Pitta

replace with zucchini for Pitta

- ½ cup cooked quinoa
- ½ cup cooked black beans
- 1 cup baby spinach
- 4 cherry tomatoes, halved
- ½ red bell pepper, diced
- ¼ cup non-GMO corn kernels
- ¼ avocado, sliced
- 2 tbsp **Cumin Lime Dressing** (see p92)

TOPPINGS: pumpkin seeds, sliced scallion (omit for Pitta), fresh cilantro

1 Spread quinoa in a wide bowl and add black beans, spinach, peppers, corn, tomatoes, and avocado.

2 Drizzle with dressing and top with pumpkin seeds, sliced scallion, and cilantro.

Six Tastes

SWEET	SOUR	SALTY	BITTER	PUNGENT	ASTRINGENT
quinoa, corn, avocado	lime (dressing), tomato	sea salt (dressing)	spinach, cilantro	scallion, bell pepper, cumin (dressing)	black beans

Tridoshic Dinners

Chakra Soups

Chakras are the seven energy centers in our body that represent specific physical and emotional aspects of our being (see pages 34–37). These chakra soups bring each chakra into balance, aligning you as your highest self.

(ROOT CHAKRA)
MULADHARA SOUP

Ground yourself with root vegetables to reconnect with Earth energy. This is perfect for when you're feeling ungrounded and need some stability.

SERVES 4

- 2 tbsp coconut oil or olive oil
- 1 medium yellow onion or fennel bulb, chopped
- 4 garlic cloves, minced (option to reduce or omit for Pitta)
- 2–3 tbsp vegan Thai red curry paste (option to omit for Pitta)
- 2 tsp ground coriander
- ½ tsp ground cumin
- ½ tsp sweet paprika
- ¼ tsp sea salt
- ¼ tsp crushed red pepper flakes (omit for Pitta)
- ⅓ cup sliced roasted red pepper
- 1 medium tomato, diced
- 3 cups cubed butternut or kabocha squash
- 1 steamed beet, cubed
- 4 cups vegetable broth
- 1 tbsp fresh lime juice
- ½ cup large unsweetened coconut flakes, toasted
- ½ cup full-fat coconut milk, to serve

1 In a large pot or Dutch oven, heat oil over medium heat. Add the onion, garlic, curry paste, coriander, cumin, paprika, salt, and red pepper flakes. Stir to combine and cook for 5 minutes, until the onion is translucent. Add the tomato and roasted red pepper and cook for 2 minutes more.

2 Add the butternut squash and beet and cook for 1 minute. Add broth and bring the mixture to a boil, then reduce heat and simmer for 15–20 minutes until the squash is soft.

3 Blend the soup to a smooth purée using an immersion blender, or let it cool and purée in batches using a regular blender. Stir in the lime juice and adjust seasoning to taste. Serve drizzled with coconut milk and sprinkled with coconut flakes.

(SACRAL CHAKRA)
SVADISTHANA BISQUE

Your sacral chakra is your ability to give and receive pleasure. Allow yourself to surrender to the spicy sweetness of this soup.

SERVES 4

- 1 large butternut squash, roasted or 2 sweet potatoes, roasted
- 1 tbsp coconut oil
- 1-in piece fresh ginger, peeled and minced
- 1 yellow onion, diced (reduce or replace with 1 fennel bulb for Pitta)
- 2 cups low-sodium vegetable stock
- 14oz can full-fat coconut milk
- 1 tsp turmeric
- ½ tsp cinnamon
- ¼ tsp sea salt
- ⅛ tsp freshly ground black pepper
- pumpkin seeds, to garnish
- hemp seeds, to garnish

1 In a large pot or Dutch oven, heat the coconut oil over medium heat. Add the ginger and onion and sauté until softened, about 3 minutes.

2 Add the stock, bring to a boil, and add the cooked butternut squash. Stir in the coconut milk, turmeric, cinnamon, salt, and pepper. Cover with lid, reduce heat to low, and let simmer for 5 minutes.

3 Blend the soup to a smooth purée using an immersion blender, or let it cool and purée in batches using a regular blender. Serve garnished with pumpkin and hemp seeds.

(SOLAR PLEXUS CHAKRA)
MANIPURA BISQUE

Who are you? Sometimes we forget. Clearing our minds with simple foods helps us remember the answer to the only question that's ever mattered.

SERVES 4

- 6 heaping cups cauliflower florets
- 3 garlic cloves, minced, or ¾ tsp asafetida
- 2 tbsp + 1 tsp grapeseed, coconut, or avocado oil, divided
- 1 tsp turmeric
- 1 tsp ground cumin
- ⅛ tsp crushed red pepper flakes (omit for Pitta)
- ½ tsp sea salt
- 1 medium yellow onion, chopped
- 3 cups vegetable broth
- ¼ cup full-fat coconut milk, to serve

1 Preheat the oven to 450°F. In a large bowl, toss the cauliflower and garlic with 2 tbsp oil until well coated. Add the turmeric, cumin, red pepper flakes, and salt. Toss well to coat evenly. Spread on a rimmed baking sheet in a single layer and roast for 25–30 minutes until browned and tender. Reserve 1 cup roasted cauliflower and set aside.

2 In a large pot or Dutch oven, heat remaining 1 tsp oil over medium heat. Add the onion and sauté for 2–3 minutes until translucent. Add the roasted cauliflower and vegetable broth. Increase heat to bring to a boil, then reduce heat, cover, and simmer for 15 minutes.

3 Blend the soup to a smooth purée using an immersion blender, or let it cool and purée in batches using a regular blender. Serve topped with reserved roasted cauliflower and a drizzle of coconut milk.

(HEART CHAKRA)
ANAHATA SOUP

There is so much more than romantic love. Love is eternal; a state of being. Filling our bodies with plants reconnects us with love's essence.

SERVES 4

- 2½ cups water
- 2 cups baby spinach leaves, packed
- 1 avocado, pitted and peeled
- ½ English cucumber, roughly chopped
- 1 small zucchini, chopped
- ½ cup mint leaves, packed
- 2 tbsp fresh lime juice, plus more to taste
- ¼ cup raw almonds, soaked overnight and drained (optional)
- ¼ tsp sea salt
- ¼ tsp freshly ground black pepper, plus more to taste
- 1 garlic clove (omit for Pitta)
- sliced watermelon radish, to garnish

1 In a blender, combine all ingredients and blend on high for 30–60 seconds until smooth and creamy. Add more water to thin out the soup if desired.

2 Taste and add more mint, lime juice, salt, and pepper to get it to your liking. Serve immediately.

(THROAT CHAKRA)
VISSUDHA SOUP

Speak your truth. When you begin, words flow out like waves in the ocean. The color blue reminds you of this.

SERVES 4

- 1 tbsp sesame, coconut, or grapeseed oil
- 2 garlic cloves, minced (reduce or omit for Pitta)
- ½ yellow onion or ½ fennel bulb, diced
- 1 large head of cauliflower, chopped
- 4 cups vegetable broth
- ¼ cup raw cashews, soaked and drained
- 2 tbsp lime
- 1 tsp blue spirulina
- ½ tsp sea salt, plus more to taste
- 2 tbsp hemp seeds, to garnish

1 In a large pot or Dutch oven, heat the oil over medium heat. Add the garlic and onion and sauté for 3 minutes until slightly brown. Add the cauliflower and sauté for 1 minute more.

2 Add the vegetable broth and increase heat to bring the mixture to a boil. Once boiling, reduce heat and simmer, uncovered, for 20–30 minutes until cauliflower is tender. Remove from heat and let cool.

3 Transfer the soup mixture to a blender with the cashews and blend on high for 1 minute until smooth and creamy.

4 Add the blue spirulina and blend briefly (excess heat from blending will diminish its nutritional value). Stir in salt to taste. Serve topped with hemp seeds.

(THIRD EYE CHAKRA)
AJNA SOUP

We have two eyes to see and a third to perceive. This indigo soup opens up your house of intuition.

SERVES 4

- 2 small purple sweet potatoes, baked
- 1 tsp coconut oil
- ½ medium yellow onion or ½ fennel bulb, diced
- ½-in piece fresh ginger, peeled and thinly sliced
- 1 cup full-fat coconut milk
- 1 cup vegetable broth or water
- 1 tbsp lemon juice
- ¼ tsp sea salt
- 1 tsp toasted sesame oil, to garnish

1 In a large pot or Dutch oven, heat coconut oil over medium heat. Add the onion and ginger and sauté for 5 minutes or until tender, stirring occasionally.

2 Whisk in the coconut milk and vegetable broth. Bring to a boil, then reduce heat and simmer for 5 minutes.

3 Scoop the sweet potato flesh from the skins and cut into ½-inch chunks. Add to the pot and cook for 5 minutes more. Remove from heat and let cool.

4 Blend the soup to a smooth purée using an immersion blender, or let it cool and purée in batches using a regular blender. Before serving, stir in lemon juice and season with salt. Serve topped with a drizzle of toasted sesame oil.

(CROWN CHAKRA)
SAHASRARA SOUP

You are tapped into a limitless source of creativity called source energy. When your crown chakra is open, that energy can flow through.

SERVES 4

3 medium red beets, tops removed

2 tsp sesame, coconut, or grapeseed oil

1 yellow onion or 1 fennel bulb, chopped

3 garlic cloves, minced (reduce or replace with ¾ tsp asafetida for Pitta)

4 cups water or vegetable broth

1 tsp freshly grated ginger

½ cup raw cashews, soaked and drained

¼ tsp turmeric

½ tsp sea salt, plus more to taste

¼ tsp freshly ground black pepper, plus more to taste

⅔ cup **Cashew Sour Cream** (see p94), to serve

1 Preheat oven to 400°F. Place beets in large Dutch oven or baking dish. Cover and roast for 1 hour until easily pierced with a fork. Let cool. Remove the skins (they should slip off easily when rubbed) and chop the beets.

2 In a large pot or Dutch oven, heat olive oil over medium heat. Add onion and sauté for 5 minutes until transparent. Add garlic and cook for 1 minute until fragrant. Stir in vegetable broth and roasted beets. Bring to a boil and cook until the beets are heated through. Remove from heat and let cool.

3 Transfer the beet mixture to a blender and purée with ginger, cashews, turmeric, salt, and pepper until smooth. Transfer puréed soup back to the soup pot over medium heat and repeat until all the soup is puréed. Serve hot, topped with a large dollop of cashew sour cream.

Chakra Meditation

Sit in a comfortable seated pose. Bring your attention to the base of your spine and imagine the color red. Move your attention to your lower belly and envision the color orange. Bring your attention to your stomach and picture the color yellow. Bring your attention to your heart and visualize the color green. Bring your attention to your throat and envisage the color blue. Bring your attention to the space between your eyebrows and think of the color indigo. Lastly, bring your attention to the top of your head and surround yourself with the color violet. Linger on any areas that feel blocked to reconnect with this chakra.

HASTI (GREEN)
Palak Tofu

People often ask me what I eat when I'm in India, and most of the time, it's this. Traditionally, this dish is called *palak paneer* and has cubes of cheese in it, but I've found that tofu is an excellent substitute. I use coconut milk instead of heavy cream, plant-based oil instead of ghee, and avoid the chilies to keep it sattvic.

SERVES 4

2 tsp olive oil

7oz firm tofu, cubed

½ tsp sea salt, divided

½ tsp ground cumin

½ tsp garam masala

½ tsp garlic powder

omit for Pitta → ½ tsp cayenne

2 tsp nutritional yeast

¼ cup water

omit for Pitta → ¼ cup full-fat coconut milk

4 garlic cloves

1-in piece fresh ginger, grated

option to omit for Pitta → 1 medium tomato, chopped

2 cups baby spinach, packed

1 tsp maple syrup (optional)

coconut cream, to serve

lime wedges, to serve

Cauliflower Rice (see p192) or **Grain-Free Naan** (see p205), to serve

1 In a large skillet, warm the olive oil over medium heat. Add the tofu to the skillet. Mix to coat and cook for 2–3 minutes. Add ¼ tsp salt, cumin, garam masala, garlic powder, cayenne, and nutritional yeast, and mix to coat. Reduce heat to medium-low and cook for 8–10 minutes, partially covered.

2 While the tofu cooks, in a blender, combine water, coconut milk, garlic, ginger, tomato, spinach, remaining ¼ tsp salt, and maple syrup (if using). Blend to a smooth purée.

3 Add the purée to the sizzling tofu and mix well. Taste and adjust seasoning as needed. Cook, covered, over medium-low heat for 10–15 minutes or until the smell of raw garlic is not detectable and desired gravy consistency is achieved. Taste and adjust seasoning as needed.

4 Before serving, drizzle with coconut cream and a squeeze of lime. Serve hot with cauliflower rice or naan.

AVAKAZA (VACATION)
Roasted Cauliflower & Lentil Tacos

Nothing says vacation like tacos. They're versatile, playful, and always satisfying—especially when they're grain-free, stuffed with plant-based goodness, and topped with a refreshing lime tahini sauce. Mucho más, mis amigos, mucho más.

SERVES 1

1 large head of cauliflower, chopped into florets

3 tbsp avocado or grapeseed oil, divided

omit for Pitta → 1 tsp garlic powder

2 tsp chili powder, divided

2 tsp ground cumin, divided

½ tsp sea salt, divided

omit or replace with ½ fennel bulb for Pitta → 1 tsp sumac (optional)

½ yellow onion, diced

2 garlic cloves, minced

1½ cups cooked green or brown lentils

reduce or omit for Pitta → 8 grain-free tortillas or **Grain-Free Chapatis** (see p204)

½ avocado, sliced

FOR THE SAUCE
⅓ cup tahini

2 tbsp lime juice

2 tbsp warm water

¼ tsp sea salt

TOPPINGS: sliced cucumber, chopped cilantro, sliced radish

1 Preheat the oven to 450°F. In a large bowl, toss the cauliflower florets with 2 tbsp oil, garlic powder, 1 tsp chili powder, 1 tsp cumin, ¼ tsp salt, and sumac (if using) until well coated. Spread in a single layer on a baking sheet and roast for 25–30 minutes until beginning to brown. Remove from oven and set aside.

2 In a medium saucepan, heat the remaining 1 tbsp oil over medium-high heat. Add the onion and garlic and sauté for 5 minutes until the onion begins to brown.

3 Add the cooked lentils and remaining 1 tsp cumin, 1 tsp chili powder, and ¼ tsp salt. Cook for 8–10 minutes, allowing the lentils to absorb the flavors. Taste and adjust seasoning as needed. Set aside.

4 To make the sauce, in a small bowl, whisk together the tahini and lime juice. Add water and salt and continue to whisk until it has reached a thick consistency.

5 To assemble, fill each tortilla with a scoop of lentils followed by some of the cauliflower florets. Top with avocado slices, drizzle generously with lime tahini sauce, and garnish with cilantro, radish, and cucumber.

VAIDZIKA (EXOTIC)
Moroccan Lentil, Chickpea & Kale Soup

The streets of a Moroccan village remind me of villages in India, with their seductive scents and colorful hodgepodge of vendors. The legume-based diet is similar, too, with harissa and paprika taking the place of turmeric and curry. Note that this richly spiced stew should be only an occasional dish for those with Pitta imbalances.

SERVES 1

2 tbsp olive oil

replace with 1 fennel bulb for Pitta → 1 yellow onion, diced

2 garlic cloves, minced

1-in piece fresh ginger, peeled and grated

1 tsp ground cumin

omit for Pitta → ½ tsp cayenne

3 carrots, diced

4 celery stalks, diced

6½ cups water or vegetable broth

1½ cups green or brown lentils

omit for Pitta → 14oz can diced tomatoes
omit for Pitta → 2 tbsp red harissa

1 tsp smoked paprika

1 tsp cinnamon

¼ tsp sea salt

¼ tsp freshly ground black pepper

2 handfuls of washed, chopped kale

15oz can chickpeas, drained and rinsed

1 tbsp fresh lemon juice

½ cup chopped fresh cilantro

Plant-Based Goat Cheese (see p135), to serve

1 In a large pot, heat olive oil over medium heat. Add the onion and sauté for 5 minutes until transparent. Add the garlic and ginger and cook for 1 minute until fragrant. Stir in the cumin, cayenne, carrot, and celery and cook for 1 minute more.

2 Add the water, lentils, tomatoes, harissa, paprika, cinnamon, salt, and pepper. Stir to combine. Increase heat and bring to a boil, then reduce heat, cover, and simmer for 30 minutes, until lentils are fully cooked.

3 Stir in the kale and chickpeas and let simmer for 5 minutes, until kale has wilted. Just before serving, stir in the lemon juice and cilantro and sprinkle plant-based goat cheese over top.

Multi-cooker: Use the sauté function to cook vegetables as directed in Step 1. Add the ingredients in Step 2 and pressure cook on high for 10 minutes. Release pressure naturally. Stir in the ingredients in Step 3 and use the sauté function to simmer for 5 minutes.

NARIKELA (COCONUT)
One-Pot Curry

The Indian state of Kerala, which is the epicenter of Ayurveda, means "land of the coconuts." There, coconuts are used for everything from meals to medicine to building products. No part of the coconut goes wasted—something we could learn from here in the West. What do you say we start a coconut revolution? I'll be here eating this coconut curry 'til you need me.

SERVES 2

1 tbsp coconut oil

½ tsp mustard seeds

2 tsp minced ginger

pinch of sea salt

omit or replace with ½ fennel bulb for Pitta → 1 medium yellow onion, diced

omit for Pitta → ½ green chile, diced

4 green cardamom pods or ¼ tsp ground cardamom

3 whole cloves or 2 tsp ground cloves

1 cinnamon stick, broken, or ½ tsp ground cinnamon

½ tsp turmeric

1 tsp garam masala

1 tsp ground corriander

¼ tsp freshly ground black pepper

1 medium tomato, chopped

4 cups chopped mixed vegetables (sweet potato, carrots, cauliflower, French green beans)

2 cups coconut milk (full-fat for Vata and Pitta; light for Kapha)

3–6 curry leaves

lime wedges, to serve

chopped fresh cilantro, to serve

Cauliflower Rice (see p192) or **Grain-Free Naan** (see p205), to serve

1 In a large pot, heat the coconut oil over medium heat. Add the mustard seeds and toast until you hear a popping sound, about 1 minute. Add the ginger, salt, onion, and green chile, if using. Sauté for 5 minutes until the onion becomes translucent.

2 Add the cardamom, cloves, cinnamon, turmeric, garam masala, coriander, and black pepper. Sauté for about 30 seconds, until the raw smell is gone.

3 Add the tomato and sauté for 1 minute. Stir in the chopped vegetables. Add the coconut milk and curry leaves, along with a pinch of salt, and stir.

4 Reduce heat to medium-low and cover. Simmer for 15 minutes until the vegetables are fully cooked.

5 Squeeze fresh lime juice over top, sprinkle with cilantro, and serve with grain-free naan or cauliflower rice, if desired.

PARICARA (FAMILY)
Plant-Based Pho

I live in Los Angeles, where driving by restaurants with names like 9021-Pho, Pho-Shizzle, Pho-King, and unPhogettable is the norm. Unfortunately, most restaurant pho is extremely high in sodium, so I don't stop. However, my plant-based version has coconut aminos, no meat products, and all the veggies. Pho-real, I think you'll like it.

SERVES 4

8 cups vegetable broth

omit for Pitta → 3 large shallots, sliced

4 garlic cloves, roughly chopped

2 whole star anise pods

3 whole cloves

2-in piece ginger, sliced

2 3-in cinnamon sticks

1 tbsp coconut aminos or tamari, plus more to taste

8oz mung bean or rice noodles

1 tbsp coconut oil

2 cups sliced shitake mushrooms

7oz extra-firm tofu, pressed and cubed

1 cup julienned carrots

OPTIONAL TOPPINGS

¼ cup chopped Thai basil

¼ cup chopped fresh cilantro

omit for Pitta → ¼ cup chopped fresh mint

¼ cup sliced scallion

2 cups mung bean sprouts

omit for Pitta → ¼ cup thinly sliced chili peppers

¼ cup slivered almonds or sunflower seeds

1 lime, cut into wedges

1 In a large pot, heat the broth, shallots, garlic, star anise, cloves, ginger, and cinnamon sticks. Bring to a simmer, then cover and let simmer for 25–30 minutes. Stir in coconut aminos, adding more if needed.

2 Cook the mung bean noodles according to package directions. Drain and rinse under cold water. Set aside.

3 In a large skillet, heat the coconut oil over medium-high heat. Add the mushrooms and tofu and sauté for 7 minutes.

4 Add the mushrooms and tofu to the broth along with the cooked noodles and carrots. Stir to combine. Simmer for 1 minute, then serve hot with your choice of toppings and a squeeze of lime.

BALAKARA (STRENGTHENING)
Sweet Potato Chickpea Burger

Stacked with healthy carbs, protein, and fats, this is the burger of your dreams and definitely the one that will convert your meat-eating friends to that #eatfeelfreshlife. Best of all, the magic sauce rivals any fast food restaurant, without any acidic eggs or even processed vegan mayo. Instead, we keep it real with our BFFs: plants.

SERVES 4

1 tbsp ground flaxseed

3 tbsp water

1 large baked sweet potato, skin removed

1½ cups cooked chickpeas

1½ cups rolled oats

1 tsp turmeric

1 tsp ground cumin

⅛ tsp freshly ground black pepper

reduce or omit for Pitta → 2–3 garlic cloves

omit for Pitta → ½ tsp cayenne

juice of ½ lemon

1 tsp apple cider vinegar

4 gluten-free seeded buns, to serve

Magic Sauce, to serve

TOPPINGS: sliced avocado, baby arugula, cilantro leaves, sliced cherry tomatoes

1 Preheat the oven to 400°F and line a baking sheet with parchment paper. Make a flax egg by mixing the ground flaxseed and water. Let sit for 15 minutes.

2 In a food processor, combine the flax egg and all remaining burger ingredients (except buns and magic sauce). Pulse until well combined.

3 Form the mixture into 4 balls and place them on the prepared baking sheet. Use a spatula to flatten the balls into patties. Place the baking sheet in the oven and bake for 25 minutes, flipping the patties once halfway through baking.

4 Serve burgers on toasted buns, topped with magic sauce, avocado, arugula, cilantro, and sliced cherry tomatoes. Enjoy your Insta-worthy burger!

MAGIC SAUCE

MAKES 1 CUP

¾ cup raw cashews, soaked and drained

½ cup water

1 tbsp apple cider vinegar

option to omit for Pitta → 1 tbsp tomato paste

1 tbsp monk fruit maple syrup or pure maple syrup

3 tsp stone-ground mustard

1 tsp turmeric

½ tsp sea salt

4 tsp pickle relish

In a food processor or blender, combine all ingredients except relish. Process until smooth, then fold in the relish. Adjust the seasoning to taste and transfer to an airtight container. Store in the fridge for up to 1 week.

ADHIKARIN (EMPOWERED)
Tempeh Tikka

Like Bollywood dancing, tikka is a staple of Indian weddings. Traditionally, vegetables and meat are marinated in yogurt and spices, then baked in a tandoor clay oven. This lighter version replaces the meat with tempeh and swaps coconut yogurt for dairy, so you'll feel light enough to dance all night.

SERVES 2

8oz package tempeh, cut into cubes

1 cup coconut yogurt

2 tbsp tandoori seasoning

¼ tsp turmeric

½ tsp ground cumin

½ tsp ground coriander

1-in piece fresh ginger, grated

½ tsp sea salt

juice of ½ lemon

3 drops liquid monk fruit sweetener or 1 tsp coconut sugar

1 tbsp sesame oil (Vata), coconut oil (Pitta), or mustard oil (Kapha), divided

omit for Pitta
1 green bell pepper, cut into 1-in pieces

1 red bell pepper, cut into 1-in pieces

1 onion, cut into 1-in pieces

1 cup broccoli florets

Cilantro Mint Chutney (see p172), to serve

Plant-Based Pink Raita (see p172), to serve

1 In a saucepan with a steamer insert, steam the tempeh for 10 minutes to soften and remove bitterness. Set aside to cool.

2 In a medium bowl, stir together the coconut yogurt, tandoori spice, turmeric, cumin, coriander, ginger, salt, lemon juice, sweetener, and oil until well combined.

3 Add the steamed tempeh to the yogurt mixture along with the red and green bell peppers, onion, and broccoli. Stir gently to ensure that tempeh and vegetables are fully coated. Cover and refrigerate for at least 1 hour to marinate.

4 Thread the tempeh cubes and sliced veggies onto skewers, leaving a little space between the pieces.

Grill method: Preheat the grill to high. Grill the skewers for 10 minutes, turning occasionally, until evenly browned.

Oven method: Preheat the oven to 375°F. Spread the skewers on a foil-lined baking sheet and bake for 15 minutes, then turn the skewers and bake on the other side for 12–15 minutes.

Stovetop method: In a large skillet, heat ½ tsp oil over medium-high heat. Pan-fry the skewers, turning frequently, about 8 minutes.

Plant-based Pink Raita—p172

cilantro mint chutney —p172

171

CILANTRO MINT CHUTNEY

It's impossible to thoroughly enjoy Indian food without a good chutney on the side. While most chutney is so spicy that I literally begin crying over dinner, this freshified version is much more mild. It gets its kick from ginger, which is soothing for the digestive system.

MAKES 2 CUPS

¼–⅓ cup water

1 bunch of fresh cilantro leaves

1 cup fresh mint leaves, packed

1 tbsp peeled, chopped fresh ginger

½–1 tsp ground cumin, to taste

juice of 1 lime

¾ tsp sea salt

4 drops liquid monk fruit sweetener or 1 tsp coconut sugar (optional)

1 In a food processor, combine all ingredients, beginning with ¼ cup water, and pulse until well-combined yet slightly chunky. For a smoother consistency, add remaining water and continue to blend. (I personally like the texture of the herbs to remain.)

2 Transfer to an airtight container and refrigerate for up to 3 days. Enjoy it with tempeh tikka, on a plant-based burger, or with anything else that may need a little green kick.

PLANT-BASED PINK RAITA

Raita is a cooling yogurt dip frequently paired with hot Indian food. This version is dairy-free and proudly pink, with creamy cashews and grounding beets.

MAKES 1¼ CUPS

1 small cucumber, peeled and grated

sea salt, to taste

1 cup raw cashews, soaked 30 minutes and drained

¾ cup water

½ cup steamed cubed beets

½ tsp cumin seeds

omit for pitta → 1 garlic clove, minced

¼ tsp ground coriander

½ tsp freshly grated ginger

juice of ½ lime

¼ cup chopped mint

1 Place the grated cucumber in a mesh strainer and sprinkle lightly with salt. Set aside to drain for a few minutes while you prepare the cashew paste.

2 In a food processor, combine the cashews, water, beets, cumin, garlic, coriander, ginger, and lime juice. Pulse until a smooth, creamy paste forms.

3 Transfer the cashew paste to a bowl and stir in the grated cucumber and chopped mint. Cover and refrigerate for 2 hours before serving, so the flavors marry. Raita can also be prepared a day or two ahead; it will become more flavorful the longer it sits.

Serve with Tempeh Tikka, Sweet Potato Turmeric Chickpea Burger, Chickpea Masala, or as a side with curries.

ANYAMANAS (VERSATILE)
GOOD-ON-EVERYTHING
COCONUT CURRY SAUCE

This sauce is so good, I could drink it on its own, but I slow myself down by eating it with roasted veggies, leafy greens, grains, legumes, tempeh tikka, or just about anything in my kitchen. It's almost as easy to make as boiling water, and you can keep it in a Mason jar to pour over everything for the next couple days.

SERVES 1

1 tbsp coconut oil (Pitta) or sesame oil (Vata, Kapha)

omit for Pitta → 1 garlic clove, minced

½-in piece fresh ginger, grated

1 tbsp curry powder

½ tsp turmeric

½ tsp garam masala

replace with light coconut milk for Kapha → 14oz can full-fat coconut milk

¼–½ tsp saffron (optional)

4 drops liquid monk fruit sweetener or 1 tsp coconut sugar

¼ tsp sea salt

juice of ½ lime

1 In a saucepan, heat the oil over medium heat. Add the garlic and ginger and sauté until golden brown, 1 minute. Add the curry powder, turmeric, and garam masala and toast for about 30 seconds.

2 Add the coconut milk, saffron, sweetener, and salt, and bring to a boil. Once boiling, reduce heat and simmer for 10–15 minutes until the desired thickness is achieved. (The longer it cooks, the thicker it will be.)

3 Remove from heat and stir in lime juice to taste. Enjoy over everything from roasted veggies to greens to tempeh tikka. Sauce can be refrigerated in an airtight container for up to 5 days.

MAHAVANA (JUNGLE) Thai Green Curry

I always want to love green curry, but sometimes the heat can be too much. Spicy foods are not recommended in Ayurveda because they overstimulate the senses and make us *rajasic*, or irritable. Instead of chilies, this green curry focuses on the refreshing flavors of the herbs and spices, which add pranic life-force to this super alkaline dish.

SERVES 4

2 tbsp coconut oil (Pitta) or sesame oil (Vata, Kapha)

½ cup **Green Curry Paste**

2 14oz cans full-fat coconut milk

4 cups chopped mixed vegetables (broccoli, cauliflower, carrots, zucchini)

juice of 2 limes

½ cup chopped cilantro, to garnish

Thai basil leaves, to garnish

1 In a large skillet, heat the oil over medium-high heat. Add the curry paste and cook for 3–4 minutes.

For extra protein, stir in ¾ cup cubed tofu with the curry paste.

2 Stir in the coconut milk and bring to a boil. Add the vegetables and reduce heat to medium. Simmer for 7–10 minutes until the veggies are tender. Remove from heat. Stir in lime juice and garnish with cilantro and Thai basil leaves.

GREEN CURRY PASTE

MAKES 1 CUP

½ cup chopped cilantro leaves

½ cup basil leaves

1 tbsp coconut aminos or tamari

1 shallot, sliced

1 lemongrass stalk, chopped, or 3 tbsp jarred lemongrass

omit for Pitta → 3 garlic cloves, middle part removed

1 tsp lime zest

1 tbsp freshly grated galangal (Thai ginger) or regular ginger

½ tsp ground coriander

½ tsp ground cumin

¾ tsp sea salt

½ tsp white pepper

2 drops liquid monk fruit sweetener or ½ tsp coconut sugar (optional)

3–4 tbsp coconut milk

Combine all ingredients in a food processor and process to a paste-like consistency. Transfer to an airtight container and refrigerate for up to 5 days.

KSANTIMAT (INDULGENT)
Spaghetti Squash
WITH LENTIL-WALNUT PLANTBALLS

Spaghetti and meatballs will forever remind me of that scene in *Lady and the Tramp*, where the two dogs accidentally kiss over a shared piece of pasta. Now you can enjoy a grain-free version of that romantic meal, topped with lentil-walnut plantballs (because why use the word "meat"?) and sugar-free tomato sauce for one heck of a date night.

SERVES 4

2 medium spaghetti squash, halved and seeded

½ tsp olive oil, melted

sea salt and freshly ground black pepper

1 cup cooked brown lentils

8oz cremini mushrooms

¼ cup walnut pieces

2 tbsp ground flaxseed

6 tbsp water

1 tbsp coconut oil

½ medium yellow onion, chopped

2 garlic cloves, chopped

2 tsp rice vinegar

1 tbsp chopped fresh sage

1 tbsp chopped fresh thyme

1 tbsp chopped fresh parsley

1 tsp dried oregano

½ cup rolled oats

2½ tbsp nutritional yeast

2 cups **Tomato Sauce** (option to omit for Pitta)

1 Preheat the oven to 375°F. Place the spaghetti squash halves face up on a baking sheet. Coat with olive oil and sprinkle with salt and pepper. Bake for 35 minutes until tender.

2 Meanwhile, make the plantballs. In a food processor, pulse the lentils, mushrooms, and walnuts until it forms a slightly lumpy mixture. Set aside. In a small bowl, mix together the ground flaxseed and water. Set aside.

3 In a large skillet, heat the coconut oil over medium heat. Add the onion and cook for 5–7 minutes until translucent. Add the garlic and cook for another 30 seconds. Stir in the rice vinegar, sage, thyme, parsley, and oregano. Cook for 1 minute more.

4 Add the mushroom-lentil mixture to the skillet and mix well. Taste and season with salt and pepper. Stir in the oats, nutritional yeast, and flax egg mixture. Transfer the mixture to a bowl to cool.

5 Once cool enough to handle, scoop and roll into golf-ball-sized balls and place in a greased muffin pan (this will help keep them moist). Bake for 30–35 minutes at 375°F until lightly browned.

6 Use a fork to scrape out the flesh of the spaghetti squash, separating it into pasta-like strands. Top with tomato sauce, if using, and the lentil-walnut plantballs. Sprinkle with fresh herbs and serve warm.

TOMATO SAUCE

MAKES 4 CUPS

1 tbsp olive oil
½ medium yellow onion, diced
3 garlic cloves, minced
28oz can crushed tomatoes
6oz can tomato paste
1 tsp dried basil
½ tsp dried oregano
3 tbsp nutritional yeast

Heat olive oil in a saucepan over medium-high heat. Add onions and garlic and sauté for 7 minutes until translucent. Stir in the crushed tomatoes and tomato paste, followed by basil, oregano, and nutritional yeast. Cook on low, barely simmering, until heated through.

KUTUMBA (FAMILY)
Cauliflower Casserole

Nothing says American family get-together like a casserole. As a kid, I saw casseroles on every TV show, and I was legitimately mad that my mom never made one. These days, I can make my own American comfort food, only I use cashews and nutritional yeast for cheesy flavor, and keep it grain free with a coconut flour topping.

SERVES 1

olive oil, for greasing

1 medium head of cauliflower, cut into florets

1 small head of broccoli, cut into florets

1 cup cooked chickpeas

1 cup chopped kale

½ cup raw cashews, soaked overnight in 2 cups filtered water

2 tsp nutritional yeast

Less for Pitta, more for Vata & Kapha → 1–3 garlic cloves, minced

2 tsp Dijon mustard

fresh basil, to garnish

FOR THE TOPPING

½ cup coconut flour

½ tsp sea salt

½ tsp dried parsley

¼ tsp onion powder

¼ tsp dried oregano

⅛ tsp freshly ground black pepper

2 tsp nutritional yeast

1 tbsp olive oil

1 Preheat the oven to 375°F and grease a 9 × 13in baking dish with olive oil. In a large saucepan with a steamer insert, lightly steam the cauliflower and broccoli florets until crisp-tender.

2 Transfer the cauliflower and broccoli to the prepared baking dish. Add the chickpeas and kale and stir to combine.

3 In a blender, combine cashews with soaking water, nutritional yeast, garlic, and mustard. Blend for 2–3 minutes until the mixture reaches a creamy consistency. Pour the sauce over the vegetables and stir to coat.

4 To make the topping, combine all ingredients in a food processor and pulse until the oil is fully incorporated and the mixture clumps together like wet sand (add more oil if needed). Spread the topping over the vegetables and bake for 15–20 minutes, until browned on top. Let cool slightly before serving, and garnish with fresh basil.

AGNI (DIGESTIVE FIRE)
Gut-Healing Seaweed Broth

Agni, the cornerstone of all things Ayurveda, is the digestive fire. We all have a fire burning inside of us, breaking down the food we eat, turning it into nutrients and discarding the waste. To keep our digestion strong, it's important to give a break now and then, and this healing broth made with kombu, a Japanese sea vegetable, is the perfect way to do that.

SERVES 4

12 cups water

1 tbsp coconut or avocado oil (Pitta) or sesame oil (Vata, Kapha)

option to omit for Pitta →

1 red onion, quartered (with skin)

2 garlic cloves, smashed

3 3-in pieces kombu

1 cup dried shitake mushrooms, sliced

1-in piece fresh ginger, chopped (with skin)

1 cup chopped carrot

1 cup chopped purple cabbage

2 celery stalks, chopped

2 cups chopped leafy greens, such as kale, spinach, collards, or bok choy

1 bay leaf

2 tbsp ground turmeric

1 tbsp coconut aminos

½ cup chopped fresh parsley, to garnish

lemon wedges, to serve

1 In a Dutch oven or large pot, combine all ingredients except parsley and lemon. Bring to a boil, then reduce heat and simmer, covered, for 1 hour. Remove from heat and let cool slightly.

2 Strain the broth in a mesh strainer, pressing down on the solids to extract all the liquid. Discard solids.

3 Serve broth garnished with freshly chopped parsley and a squeeze of lemon. Broth can be refrigerated in an airtight container for up to 1 week, or frozen for up to 1 month. Reheat on stovetop to serve.

Multi-cooker: Combine all ingredients except parsley and lemon. Pressure cook on high for 10 minutes. Let pressure release naturally for another 10 minutes, then release pressure manually. Strain solids.

SATTVIC (PURE)
Tridoshic Kitchari

We keep it sattvic in the *Eat Feel Fresh* kitchen—light, pure, and super high vibe. We live in crazy times with crazy schedules and the best thing we can do for our bodies is keep it simple. Kitchari is considered the most healing food in Ayurveda because it's so easy to digest, giving the system a break to restore. Kitchari is like a reset for your gut and best of all—it's delicious.

SERVES 4

Less for Pitta, more for Vata & Kapha →

2 tbsp sesame oil (Vata, Kapha) or coconut oil (Pitta)

→ 1–2 tsp cumin seeds

2 tsp fennel seeds

1 tsp mustard seeds

2 tsp ground coriander

Less for Pitta, more for Vata & Kapha → ½–1-in piece fresh ginger, grated

1 tsp turmeric powder

¼ tsp asafetida (optional)

7 cups water

1 cup basmati rice, soaked overnight, rinsed, and drained

1 cup split yellow mung beans (dhal), soaked overnight, rinsed, and drained

½ tsp sea salt

1 tsp chopped fresh cilantro, to serve

juice of 1 lime, to serve

ground flaxseed, to serve

Vata
½ cup diced sweet potato

1 cup chopped mustard greens

Pitta
½ cup chopped kale

½ cup diced butternut squash

2 tbsp coconut cream

Kapha
½ cup cauliflower florets

1 cup chopped dandelion greens

1 In a Dutch oven, heat the oil over medium heat. Add the cumin, fennel, and mustard seeds and cook for 3 minutes or until the mustard seeds begin to pop. Add the coriander, ginger, turmeric, and asafetida (if using). Stir to combine.

2 Stir in the water, rice, mung beans, and vegetables for your Dosha. Bring the mixture to a boil, then reduce the heat and simmer, stirring occasionally, until rice and mung beans are cooked and vegetables are soft, 40–50 minutes.

3 Season with salt to taste. Serve warm, topped with fresh cilantro, lime juice, and a sprinkle of ground flaxseed. Kitchari can be refrigerated in an airtight container for up to 4 days.

Multi-cooker: Use the sauté function to heat spices, then add water, rice, mung beans, and vegetables and pressure cook on high for 15 minutes. Release pressure manually.

PARIHASA (FUN)
Sweet Potato Pesto Pizza

Pizza just got a plant-based, Ayurvedic upgrade with a root veggie crust, dairy-free pesto, almond feta, and assorted veggie toppings. Better yet, it contains the six tastes: sweet (sweet potatoes), sour (lemon), salty (salt), bitter (arugula), pungent (curry), and astringent (walnuts), leaving you satiated and craving-free. Best of all, there are no tomatoes—perfect for Pittas!

SERVES 2

1 cup mashed sweet potato

1 cup oat flour (blended oats)

1 tsp baking soda

½ tsp dried oregano

½ tsp dried basil

½ tsp sea salt

⅛ tsp freshly ground black pepper

¼ tsp curry powder (optional)

OPTIONAL TOPPINGS

¼ cup **Plant-Based Pesto** (see p95)

Almond Feta (see p139)

Roasted Chickpeas (see p196)

your choice of veggies (such as mushrooms, kale, artichoke hearts)

handful of arugula, tossed in olive oil and lemon juice (optional)

1 Preheat the oven to 400°F. In a large bowl, combine the sweet potato, oat flour, baking soda, oregano, basil, salt, pepper, and curry powder, if using. Knead well, until the mixture forms a well-blended but still somewhat sticky dough.

2 Spread a sheet of parchment paper on a work surface and dust with oat flour. Use a rolling pin to roll the dough into a large circle, about 10 inches in diameter and ½ inch thick.

3 Transfer the parchment paper and dough to a baking sheet. Bake for 15–20 minutes or until the edges are slightly browned.

4 Remove the crust from the oven. Spread pesto over the crust, then top with almond feta, roasted chickpeas, and vegetables. Broil for 3–5 minutes or until the vegetables begin to brown. Cool briefly before slicing. Top with dressed arugula and enjoy.

ILAVA (FARMER)
Sweet Potato Lentil Shepherd's Pie

The name "shepherd's pie" doesn't exactly scream "sexy," but not everything has to. This is more of a cozy sweater, fuzzy socks, reading in front of the fireplace dinner, and who doesn't love that? Total Kapha mood. It's an easy recipe to throw together if you've got lentils and sweet potatoes and want to transform them into something really out-of-the-bowl.

SERVES 8

4 large sweet potatoes, quartered

1 tbsp olive oil

½ cup diced onion

½ cup diced celery

½ cup diced carrot

3 garlic cloves, minced

4½ cups cooked brown lentils

2 15oz cans diced tomatoes

2 tbsp coconut aminos or tamari

1 tbsp chopped fresh basil

1 tsp fresh thyme, plus more to garnish

½ cup chopped spinach

2 tbsp non-dairy milk, plus more as needed

sea salt and freshly ground black pepper, to taste

1 Preheat the oven to 425°F. Place potatoes in a large pot of water and boil for 15–20 minutes until soft.

2 Meanwhile, in a Dutch oven, heat the olive oil over medium heat. Add the onion, celery, and carrots and cook, stirring occasionally, for 10 minutes or until soft. Add the garlic and cook for 1 minute. Add the lentils and cook for 3 minutes more. Stir in the diced tomatoes, basil, spinach, and coconut aminos. Simmer for 10–15 minutes.

3 When the sweet potatoes are soft, remove them from the heat and drain the water. Remove the potato skins and return the potatoes to the pot. Add the non-dairy milk and mash with a fork or potato masher until smooth and thick, adding more non-dairy milk if needed. Season with salt and pepper to taste.

4 Spread the lentil mixture in a greased 9 × 13in baking dish. Spread the sweet potatoes in an even layer over top. Bake for 20 minutes. Allow to cool slightly before serving and garnish with thyme.

If using a Dutch oven, sweet potatoes can be spread directly over lentils and placed in the oven.

ATMAN (SOUL)
Yellow Daal Tadka

To make this staple Indian dish of cooked split peas, aromatic spices are tempered in hot oil to bring out their flavor and nutritional benefits. Wait until you hear the popping sound of the mustard seeds, which aid the digestive process and reduce gas associated with legumes. I like making this sattvic style: onion and garlic free.

SERVES 4

2 tbsp coconut oil (Pitta) or sesame oil (Vata, Kapha)

1 tsp cumin seeds

1 tsp brown mustard seeds

1 small tomato, chopped

1-in piece ginger, peeled and minced

½ tsp ground turmeric

1 tsp curry powder

½ tsp ground coriander

½ tsp sea salt, plus more to taste

⅛ tsp freshly ground black pepper

 optional for more pungency → ¼ tsp asafetida powder

1 cup yellow split peas, rinsed, soaked, and drained

3½ cups water

2 cups chopped spinach

juice of ½ lime

¼ cup chopped cilantro, to garnish

Grain-Free Naan (see p205), to serve

1 In a Dutch oven or large pot, heat the oil over medium-high heat. Add the cumin and mustard seeds, and cook for about 1 minute until you hear them begin to pop.

2 Add the chopped tomato and cook for 1 minute. Add the ginger, turmeric, curry powder, coriander, salt, pepper, and asafetida (if using). Reduce heat to medium and cook for 1 minute.

3 Stir in the split peas and water and bring to a boil. Reduce heat and simmer for 45 minutes until peas are soft enough to mash.

4 Using a spoon or whisk, mash the peas. Once the daal reaches a smooth consistency, stir in the spinach and cook for 5 minutes until wilted.

5 Top with cilantro and fresh lime juice and serve with a side of naan (if desired).

KALADVIPIYA (AFRICAN)
Sun-Butter & Root Vegetable Soup

While traveling in Zimbabwe, I fell in love with *dovi*, a traditional dish comprised of peanut butter, spices, and vegetables—basically, my life in a bowl. I recreated it with sunflower seed butter, which offers twice as much fiber and just as much protein as peanut butter, is mold-free, and has a way better fatty acid profile. Yes, you can have thirds.

SERVES 4

2 tbsp coconut oil

replace with 1 tsp asafetida for Pitta → 4 garlic cloves, minced

1 medium yellow onion, diced

replace with 1 fennel bulb for Pitta → 1- to 2-in piece fresh ginger, peeled and grated

1 large sweet potato, peeled and cubed

1 large carrot, chopped

2 celery stalks, chopped

1 tsp turmeric

1 tsp ground coriander

½ tsp ground cumin

¼ tsp cinnamon

⅓ tsp fenugreek

¼ tsp cayenne pepper

1 tbsp coconut aminos or tamari (optional)

omit for Pitta → 3 tbsp tomato paste

¾ cup sunflower seed butter

4 cups low-sodium vegetable broth or water

1½ cups cooked chickpeas

½ bunch collard greens, chopped

¼ tsp sea salt

fresh cilantro, to garnish

sunflower seeds, to garnish

1 In a Dutch oven or large pot, heat the oil over medium-high heat. Add the garlic, onion, and ginger, and sauté for 5 minutes until soft. Add the sweet potato, carrot, celery, spices, and coconut aminos and sauté for 1 minute more.

2 Add the tomato paste, sunflower seed butter, and vegetable broth. Bring to a boil, then reduce heat to medium-low. Simmer for 25 minutes, covered, until the sweet potatoes are soft.

3 Using the back of a spoon, smash some of the sweet potato to thicken the stew. Stir in the chickpeas and collard greens and simmer for 5 minutes more. Season with salt and serve garnished with cilantro and sunflower seeds.

Multi-cooker: Use the sauté function to cook vegetables as directed in Step 1. Add the ingredients in Step 2 and pressure cook on high for 10 minutes. Let the pressure release naturally. Stir in the ingredients in Step 3 and use the sauté function to simmer.

PARAMPARIKA (TRADITIONAL)
Masala Chickpea Bowl

This dish is perfect for a cold winter day, especially for Vata and Kapha constitutions. The activated mustard seeds make it super easy to digest, and the array of spices really rev up the digestive fire. Because it's so warming, Pittas should only eat it occasionally, and load up on leafy greens before and after to balance out the heat.

SERVES 4

replace with 1 fennel bulb for Pitta

optional for Pitta

1 tbsp coconut oil
1 tbsp mustard seeds
1 tsp cumin seeds
1 onion, diced
2–3 garlic cloves, minced
5 medium tomatoes, diced
14oz can full-fat coconut milk
1 tbsp freshly grated ginger
1 tsp garam masala
1 tsp turmeric
1 tsp ground coriander
1 tsp curry powder
¼ tsp asafetida (optional)
3 cups cooked chickpeas (two 15oz cans)
2 cups cooked black quinoa
2 cups steamed kale
3 tbsp hemp seeds, to garnish

1 In a large skillet, heat the coconut oil over medium-high heat. Add the mustard and cumin seeds. Heat for 1 minute, or until the seeds begin to sizzle and pop. Add the onion or fennel and garlic, if using. Reduce heat to medium and cook for 5 minutes, until the onions are soft and translucent.

2 Add the tomatoes and cook for 2 minutes. Stir in the coconut milk, ginger, garam masala, turmeric, coriander, curry powder, and asafetida, if using. Reduce heat to medium-low and simmer for 20 minutes until slightly thickened. Add the chickpeas. Let simmer, covered, for 5 minutes. Remove from heat and let sit for 5 minutes.

3 Serve over cooked quinoa with a side of steamed kale, and garnish with a sprinkle of hemp seeds.

Snacks and Sides

ADHUNIKA (MODERN)
Cauliflower Rice

A quick pulse in the food processor transforms raw cauliflower into rice-sized pieces that can replace regular rice in any dish. Ayurveda is extremely rice-based, so this is a great way to lighten the load with fewer carbohydrates and calories and more micronutrient-rich plants. Here are three of my favorite ways to prepare cauliflower rice, each with unique medicinal benefits. Eat your prescription!

CILANTRO LIME (DETOXIFYING AND ALKALIZING)

MAKES 4 CUPS

1 head of cauliflower, cut into florets

1 tbsp sesame oil (Vata, Kapha) or coconut oil (Pitta)

½ yellow onion, diced

2 garlic cloves, minced

1 medium lime (zest and juice)

¼ cup chopped fresh cilantro

½ tsp sea salt

1 Place cauliflower in a food processor and process until broken down to a rice-like texture. (This will create about 4 cups riced cauliflower.)

2 In a large skillet, heat oil over medium heat. Add the onion and cook for 4–5 minutes or until translucent. Add the garlic and cook until fragrant, about 1 minute more.

3 Add the riced cauliflower to the pan and cook for 5–7 minutes, stirring frequently, until the cauliflower is slightly crispy on the outside and tender on the inside.

4 Remove from heat and stir in the lime zest, cilantro, and salt to taste. Squeeze fresh lime juice over the rice before serving.

SAFFRON (HORMONE-BALANCING AND MOOD-BOOSTING)

MAKES 4 CUPS

1 tsp saffron threads

1 head of cauliflower, cut into florets

1 tbsp sesame oil (Vata, Kapha) or coconut oil (Pitta)

½ yellow onion, diced

3 garlic cloves, minced

2 tbsp vegetable broth

½ tsp sea salt

1 Crumble the saffron threads into a small, stain-proof bowl. Add 1 tbsp hot water and let saffron soak while you prepare the dish.

2 Place cauliflower in a food processor and process until broken down to a rice-like texture. (This will create about 4 cups riced cauliflower.)

3 In a large skillet, heat oil over medium heat. Add the onion and cook for 4–5 minutes or until translucent. Add the garlic and cook until fragrant, about 1 minute more.

4 Add the riced cauliflower to the pan, and cook for 5–7 minutes, until tender. Add the saffron (with soaking water), broth, and salt. Stir well, and cook for 1 minute more before serving.

CURRY GINGER (DIGESTIVE-ENHANCING AND WARMING)

MAKES 4 CUPS

1 head of cauliflower, cut into florets

1 tbsp sesame oil (Vata, Kapha) or coconut oil (Pitta)

2 tsp curry powder

¼ tsp turmeric

½ tsp ground ginger

½ tsp sea salt

4 tbsp chopped fresh parsley

1 Place cauliflower in a food processor and process until broken down to a rice-like texture. (This will create about 4 cups riced cauliflower.)

2 In a large skillet, heat oil over medium heat. Once hot, add the riced cauliflower and cook for 5 minutes, until soft.

3 Stir in the curry powder, turmeric, ginger, and salt, and cook for 1–2 minutes more, until fragrant. Sprinkle with fresh parsley before serving.

DHAYAS (REFRESHING)
QUINOA TABBOULEH SALAD

Growing up I loved tabbouleh salad. And when I say "love," I mean I would get a family-size container and finish it all by myself in one go. However, the bulgur in traditional tabbouleh contains a lot of gluten, which my body is sensitive to. I decided to swap it out for quinoa, which tastes like a grain but is actually a protein-rich seed. Now I can enjoy my tabbouleh with extra herbs, less tomato, and zero gluten.

MAKES 5 CUPS

omit for Pitta →

reduce or omit for Pitta →

2 cups water
1 cup quinoa
½ cup chopped scallion
1 medium tomato, chopped, seeds removed
1 Persian cucumber, diced
1 cup finely chopped mint (1 bunch)
2 cups finely chopped parsley (2 bunches)
juice of 2 lemons
4 tbsp extra virgin olive oil
½ tsp sea salt
½ tsp ground cumin (optional)

1 Rinse the quinoa with cool water. In a saucepan, bring 2 cups water to a boil over high heat. Stir in the quinoa, reduce heat, cover, and simmer for 15 minutes or until all the water has been absorbed. Let the quinoa cool before preparing the salad.

2 In a large bowl, combine the cooled, cooked quinoa with the scallion, tomato, cucumber, mint, and parsley. Stir in the lemon juice, olive oil, salt, and cumin, if using. Taste and adjust seasoning as needed.

For more flavor, add dried herbs, sea salt, lemon juice, or apple cider vinegar to the boiling water before stirring in the quinoa.

"If you don't take care of your health today, you will be forced to take care of your illness tomorrow."

—DR. DEEPAK CHOPRA

ZITAKRIYA (COOLING) CILANTRO LIME RICE

Not only is cilantro refreshing, but it draws heavy metals out of your system, which many of us are unknowingly carrying. Sneak it into your rice for detoxifying benefits.

MAKES 3 CUPS

½ tbsp olive oil
1 cup brown or basmati rice
2 cups water or vegetable broth
1 medium lime (zest and juice)
¼ cup chopped cilantro
½ tsp sea salt

1 In a medium saucepan, heat oil over medium heat. Add the rice and lime zest and cook, stirring occasionally, for 3–5 minutes until toasted.

2 Stir in the water (or vegetable broth) and bring to a boil. Once boiling, reduce heat, cover, and simmer for 20–25 minutes or until the liquid has been absorbed.

3 Remove from heat and stir in lime juice, cilantro, and salt to taste. Rice can be stored in an airtight container for up to 5 days.

DVIPA (ISLAND) COCONUT LIME QUINOA

Some people aren't a fan of plain quinoa, but when flavored correctly, it's a whole other experience. Coconut and lime offer a tropical vibe, making you feel like you're on the beaches of Kerala, India.

MAKES 3 CUPS

2 cups coconut milk (any variety)
1 cup quinoa
2 limes (zest and juice)

1 In a medium saucepan, combine coconut milk, quinoa, and lime juice. Bring to a boil, then cover and reduce heat. Simmer for 12–15 minutes until all the liquid has been absorbed.

2 Remove from the heat, stir, and let stand until cool. Stir in the zest of both limes and serve either as is or slightly reheated. Quinoa can be refrigerated in an airtight container for up to 5 days.

ALPAHARA (SNACK)
Roasted Chickpeas

I like to keep roasted chickpeas on hand for some extra excitement in my Six-Taste Bowls/life. Depending on my mood, I'll dress them up with refreshing Mediterranean herbs, sizzling chipotle pepper, earthy cumin, nutty sesame and garlic, or sweet and spicy cinnamon, so it's like an instant vacation with every bite. (Well, not quite—but definitely makes my lunch a little more exotic!)

SERVES 2

1 tbsp grapeseed oil (can also use coconut, avocado, or sesame oil)
2 cups cooked chickpeas
flavoring blend of choice

1 Preheat the oven to 350°F. Line a baking sheet with parchment paper or lightly oiled foil.

2 Place the chickpeas on a clean kitchen towel or a few paper towels and gently pat them dry (the drier they are, the crisper they will become when roasted). Remove any loose skins.

3 In a medium bowl, combine the oil with your choice of flavorings and whisk until fully combined. Add the chickpeas and mix thoroughly, ensuring chickpeas are evenly coated.

4 Spread the chickpeas on the prepared baking sheet in a single layer. Bake for 1 hour, stirring and tossing the chickpeas halfway through cooking. Before removing from the oven, check to make sure the chickpeas are crunchy. Chickpeas will become crunchier as they cool.

For extra crunchiness, turn off the oven and leave the chickpeas inside to dry for 30–40 minutes, checking every 10 minutes to ensure they haven't burned.

MEDITERRANEAN HERB
2 tsp apple cider vinegar
2 tsp lemon juice
1 tsp sea salt
1 tsp dried oregano
½ tsp garlic powder
½ tsp freshly ground black pepper

← option to omit for Pitta

MEXICAN CHIPOTLE
1 garlic clove, minced

1-in piece chipotle chile in adobo, minced

1 tsp adobo sauce

¼ tsp chipotle chili powder

½ tsp ground cumin

½ tsp sea salt

freshly ground black pepper, to taste

option to omit for Pitta

INDIAN MASALA
1 tbsp lemon juice

1 tsp ground cumin

½ tsp ground coriander

½ tsp cayenne pepper *option to omit for Pitta*

½ tsp sea salt

¼ tsp cinnamon

ASIAN SESAME GARLIC
1 tbsp sesame oil

½ tsp garlic powder *option to omit for Pitta*

½ tsp sea salt

2 tsp sesame seeds

1 tsp coconut aminos or tamari

CINNAMON TOAST
1 tbsp coconut oil

2 tbsp monk fruit maple syrup

1 tsp cinnamon

¼ tsp sea salt

LAGHUPAKA (EASY DIGESTION) LOW-FODMAP SALSA

FODMAPs are a type of carbohydrate found in many foods, such as onion and garlic, which can cause digestive discomfort and IBS. Coincidently, onion and garlic also aren't recommended for Pittas and those on yogic-paths. This salsa recipe is your new digestive-friendly party staple.

MAKES 2 CUPS

6 very ripe red tomatoes, diced
1 medium green bell pepper, diced
¼ cup chopped fresh chives
¼ cup chopped fresh cilantro
¼ cup chopped fresh or dried parsley (optional)
¼–½ cup diced scallions, green part only
juice of 1 lime
1 tsp sea salt
½–1 tsp chili powder   *← option to omit for Pitta*
   or 1–2 green chilies, chopped

1 In a large bowl, combine all ingredients and stir well. Taste and adjust seasoning as needed. (If desired, you can process the salsa in a food processor or blender for a smoother consistency.)

2 Transfer to an airtight container. Salsa can be refrigerated for up to 5 days.

PRAHARA (HEATING) CUMIN GUACAMOLE

In Ayurveda, onions and garlic are considered rajasic, meaning they lower consciousness by creating more agitation in your energy. They also imbalance Pitta, the fire Dosha, which can lead to heartburn and inflammation in the system. You can keep vibing high with this onion- and garlic-free guacamole that will tantalize your taste buds with savory cumin, which aids digestion, boosts the immune system, and promotes skin glow.

MAKES 1½ CUPS

2 ripe avocados
juice of ½ lime, plus more if needed
1 tsp ground cumin
½ tsp chili powder   *option to omit for Pitta →*
¼ tsp sea salt
1 tomatillo, chopped   *← replace with 2 tbsp unsweetened coconut flakes for Pitta*
3 tbsp chopped fresh cilantro

1 Halve and pit the avocados and scoop the flesh into a large bowl. Add the lime juice, cumin, chili powder, salt, and pepper. Mash the mixture with a fork into a coarse texture. Taste and adjust seasoning as needed.

2 Fold in the tomatoes and cilantro. Cover and refrigerate for 1 hour before serving.

APURANA (SATIATING) AVOCADO TAHINI DIP

I'm obsessed with tahini, the nut-free ground sesame seed butter with a rich texture and earthy, nutty flavor. Pair it with avocado, and you get a great combination for improving skin health and boosting nutrient absorption, which we all could use a little more of. Once you make this dip, you'll want to devour it in one go. Pro tip: use some cucumbers as a vehicle to pace yourself.

MAKES ¾ CUP

1 large ripe avocado, pitted
2 tbsp tahini
juice of ½ lemon
½ garlic clove, minced ← *option to omit for Pitta*
½ tsp sea salt
½ tsp cumin

TOPPINGS: olive oil, fresh cilantro, pepitas

1 Using a mortar and pestle or food processor, combine all ingredients. Blend until it reaches your desired consistency. Taste and adjust seasoning as needed.

2 Serve topped with a swirl of olive oil, freshly chopped cilantro, and pepitas.

SAUVARNA (GOLDEN) TURMERIC SWEET POTATO HUMMUS

Sweet potato and turmeric take yet another twist—this time in a creamy, golden hummus. This grounding yet stimulating dip is balancing for all three Doshas.

MAKES 3 CUPS

1 medium sweet potato, baked and skin removed
2 cups cooked chickpeas or white beans
3 tbsp tahini
1 tsp turmeric
½ tsp ground cumin
½ tsp sweet paprika   *Less for Pitta,*
1–3 garlic cloves ← *more for Vata and Kapha*
juice of 1 lemon
zest of ½ lemon
1 tbsp light sesame oil (Vata, Kapha) or olive oil (Pitta)
sea salt and freshly ground pepper, to taste

1 In a food processor, combine the sweet potato, chickpeas, tahini, turmeric, cumin, paprika, garlic, lemon juice, and lemon zest. Process until combined. With the machine running, stream in oil until smooth and creamy. Season with salt and pepper to taste.

2 Transfer to an airtight container. Hummus can be refrigerated for up to 5 days.

PRERAKA (STIMULATING)
Ginger Edamame Hummus

Hummus is every plant-based person's bestie, but I'm going to be honest—sometimes it can get a bit boring. Why not mix it up with some ginger and edamame? Ginger enhances your *agni*, digestive fire, making it perfect for those who may have a bit of a hard time with beans. Edamame is high in protein and contains isoflavones, which are incredible for healthy skin, bones, and immune system.

MAKES 1 CUP

1 cup cooked pre-shelled edamame (frozen and thawed is fine)

¼ cup tahini

½-in piece ginger, peeled and chopped (about ½ tbsp)

2 tbsp lemon juice

1 garlic clove, peeled (option to omit for Pitta)

¼ cup chopped fresh cilantro (optional)

2 tbsp olive oil

¼ tsp sea salt

1 In a food processor or high-powered blender, combine all ingredients and blend until smooth. (Add more olive oil for a creamier consistency.) Taste and add more salt if needed.

2 Transfer to an airtight container and refrigerate for up to 5 days.

HEMALLA (WINTER) TANDOORI CAULIFLOWER DIP

Tandoori spices are a staple in every Ayurvedic kitchen. They rev up the *agni*, digestive fire, increase nutrient absorbability, reduce bloating and gas, and eliminate *ama*, toxins from the system. Plus, they're delicious.

MAKES 3 CUPS

1 head of cauliflower, chopped into florets
2 tbsp olive oil
2 tbsp + 2 tsp tandoori seasoning, divided
⅔ cup unsweetened plain coconut yogurt
juice of 1 lemon
¼ tsp sea salt
⅛ tsp freshly ground black pepper *← omit for Pitta*

TOPPINGS: fresh parsley, lime wedges, **Roasted Chickpeas** (see p196)

1 Preheat the oven to 400°F. In a medium bowl, toss the cauliflower with olive oil and 2 tbsp tandoori seasoning. Spread the cauliflower on a parchment-paper lined baking sheet and roast in oven for 20 minutes. Remove and let cool.

2 In a food processor or blender, combine the roasted cauliflower, remaining 2 tsp tandoori seasoning, coconut yogurt, lemon juice, salt, and pepper. Blend until smooth.

3 Garnish with fresh parsley, lime wedges, and roasted chickpeas before serving, and enjoy with steamed vegetables or raw vegan crackers. Store in airtight container in refrigerator for up to 4 days.

AVAPATA (FALL) PUMPKIN HUMMUS

Not all hummus has to have chickpeas! Sometimes your belly needs a little break from the legumes, and that's when you come to this smooth and creamy recipe. It contains all six tastes—sweet pumpkin, sour lemon, bitter zucchini and olive oil, pungent garlic and cumin, and astringent tahini and pumpkin seeds— keeping your body satisfied and craving-free.

MAKES 1½ CUPS

1 medium zucchini, peeled and roughly chopped
1 cup pumpkin purée
¼ cup tahini
1–2 tbsp extra virgin olive oil *← less for Kapha, more for Vata and Pitta*
1 garlic clove, minced
juice of 1 lemon *← omit for Pitta*
1 tsp ground cumin
½ tsp paprika
½ tsp sea salt
½ tsp chili powder *← omit for Pitta*
raw pumpkin seeds, to garnish

1 In a food processor or blender, combine all ingredients except pumpkin seeds and process until smooth. Taste and adjust seasonings as desired.

2 Top with pumpkin seeds before serving, and enjoy with steamed vegetables. Store in an airtight container in the refrigerator for up to 4 days.

*"When diet is wrong, medicine is of no use;
when diet is correct, medicine is of no need."*

-AYURVEDIC PROVERB

PRTHVI (EARTH ELEMENT)
CHAI PUMPKIN PIE BUTTER

This is the perfect spread or dip for the cold and dry Vata season. Pumpkin grounds that overactive Vata energy, while chai spices heat up your body from within. Walnuts are an excellent source of healthy fat and boost bone health, which is especially needed during Vata season when your joints are cracking like sparklers.

MAKES 2 CUPS

1½ cups walnuts, toasted

15oz can organic pumpkin purée or 2 cups roasted pumpkin

1 tsp cinnamon

½ tsp freshly grated ginger

½ tsp ground nutmeg

½ tsp ground cloves

¼ tsp sea salt

1 tbsp monk fruit maple syrup or another sweetener

1 In a food processor, pulse the walnuts a few times to a coarse consistency. Add all remaining ingredients and process until smooth, 1–3 minutes.

2 Enjoy spread on a piece of sprouted-grain toast, stirred into your Om-meal, with sliced apples, or with a banana. Store in airtight container in refrigerator for up to 1 week.

MAHANASA (KITCHEN)
Grain-Free Chapati

Chapati is a type of unleavened flatbread consumed with almost every Indian meal. Unlike naan, it's thin and pancake-like, cooked on a *tawa*, or flat griddle, in the home, while naan is cooked in a *tandoor*, or clay naan. This chapati is made with nutrient-dense, low-glycemic coconut flour and arrowroot starch instead of wheat flour, making it a much healthier option.

MAKES 4

¼ cup coconut flour

½ cup arrowroot starch

1 cup full-fat coconut milk or water

1 tsp apple cider vinegar

½ tsp sea salt

¼ tsp freshly ground black pepper

½ tbsp coconut oil

1 In a small bowl, mix together coconut flour, arrowroot starch, coconut milk, vinegar, and salt until well combined. Let sit for 10 minutes.

2 In a medium skillet, heat coconut oil over medium-high heat. Once hot, spoon ¼ cup of the batter into the pan and use the back of the spoon to spread it into a circle.

3 Cook for 3-4 minutes, until bubbles begin to appear on the surface and the edges begin to brown. Flip and cook for another 2–3 minutes.

4 Repeat with the remaining batter, transfering the chapati to a plate lined with paper towel as they are cooked. Serve with raita, chutney, or curry. I recommend eating these immediately, as they taste best fresh.

BHARATAVARSIYA (INDIAN)
Grain-Free Naan

If naan ran for president, it would win. Naan is the fluffy Indian bread that accompanies every curry. However, it's usually made with refined wheat, which causes digestive issues and feeds candida. I sought to create a grain-free version that epitomizes everything *Eat Feel Fresh* is about, and this recipe just about nails it. You won't need to order Indian takeout any longer!

MAKES 4

½ cup almond flour
½ cup tapioca starch or arrowroot starch
1 tsp apple cider vinegar
1 tsp garlic powder
1 tsp sea salt
½ tsp freshly ground black pepper
1 cup full-fat coconut milk
2 tbsp sesame or coconut oil, for pan

1 In a medium bowl, whisk together the almond flour, tapioca starch, vinegar, garlic powder, salt, and pepper. Stir in the coconut milk, mixing well to combine.

2 In a medium skillet, heat ½ tbsp oil over medium-high heat. Pour in ¼ cup of the batter and swirl around slightly. Cook for 3–4 minutes, until it begins to look golden. Flip and cook for another 2–3 minutes until edges are crisp.

3 Repeat with the remaining batter. Serve immediately with raita, chutney, or curry—these taste best when freshly made.

Desserts

LAKSHMI (GODDESS OF ABUNDANCE)
Raw Rose & Pistachio Cheesecake

The Hindu goddess Lakshmi, representing wealth and fertility, was supposedly born from 108 large rose petals and 1,008 small rose petals. This dairy-free cheesecake is an offering to her grace and beauty, in gratitude for her fruitful blessings of abundance.

SERVES 12

FOR THE CRUST
1 cup raw almonds
8 dates, pitted
1 tbsp coconut oil
1 tsp cinnamon

FOR THE PISTACHIO LAYER
½ cup raw cashews, soaked overnight, rinsed, and drained
½ cup raw, shelled pistachios, soaked overnight, rinsed, and drained
16 drops liquid monk fruit sweetener
1 tsp alcohol-free vanilla extract
¼ tsp spirulina (for color)
½ tbsp lemon juice
2 tbsp melted coconut oil

FOR THE ROSE LAYER
1 cup raw cashews, soaked overnight, rinsed, and drained
4 tbsp maple syrup
2 tsp rose water
1 tbsp lemon juice
1 tbsp raspberry powder
½ tsp beet root powder (for color)
⅛ tsp sea salt
2 tbsp melted coconut oil

1 To make the crust, place all the ingredients in a food processor and blend on high until a sticky, well-combined crumb is formed. Test crust by rolling a small amount of the mixture in your hands. If the ingredients hold together, your crust is perfect. If the crust is too dry, add water 1 tbsp at a time to achieve the right consistency.

2 Spread the mixture evenly in an 8-inch springform pan, pressing down to form a flat base layer. Place in the freezer for 10 minutes to set while you prepare the pistachio layer.

3 To make the pistachio layer, place all ingredients in a blender and blend on high until smooth. Remove the crust from the freezer and spread the pistachio layer evenly over top. Return it to the freezer for 20 minutes to set while you prepare the rose layer.

4 To make the rose layer, place all the ingredients in a blender and blend on high until smooth. Once the pistachio layer has set, remove the pan from the freezer and spread the rose layer evenly over top. Cover with foil and return to the freezer for 4 hours until frozen and firmly set.

5 Once the cake has completely set, release it from the pan and let sit at room temperature for a few minutes to warm before slicing.

SARJANATMAKA (CREATIVE)
Mung Bean Brownies

Mung beans are about as Ayurvedic as it gets. The reason we love them so much is because they're the easiest of all legumes to digest. This recipe is like the dessert version of kitchari, minus the pungent spices, plus some cacao lovin'.

SERVES 9

1½ cups cooked mung beans

½ cup cacao powder

½ cup quick oats

20 drops liquid monk fruit sweetener or 6-8 pitted Medjool dates

2 tbsp melted coconut oil

2 tsp alcohol-free vanilla extract

½ tsp baking powder

¼ tsp sea salt

½ cup dairy-free dark chocolate chips, plus more for topping

1 Preheat the oven to 350°F. Line an 8 × 8in baking pan with parchment paper.

2 In a food processor or blender, combine all ingredients except for the chocolate chips and blend until smooth.

3 Stir in the chocolate chips and spread the batter evenly in the prepared baking pan. (Batter will be a little crumbly, but that's fine.) Sprinkle additional chocolate chips over top.

4 Bake for 16–20 mins until a toothpick inserted in the center comes out clean. Immediately after removing the pan from the oven, use an offset spatula to spread the melted chocolate chips over the brownies. Allow to cool before slicing. Store in an airtight container in the fridge for up to 3 days.

ZAKTI (STRENGTH)
Chickpea Cookie Dough

Cookie dough has got to be my (and everyone's) favorite dessert, but it doesn't leave you feelin' very fresh when you've polished off half a tub. This version uses protein-rich chickpeas as a base, paired with creamy, dreamy sunflower seed butter and sugar-free monk fruit sweetener. All the zakti strength, none of the salmonella.

MAKES 2 CUPS

1½ cups cooked chickpeas or white beans, rinsed and patted dry

¼ cup sunflower seed butter

2 tbsp non-dairy milk, plus more as needed

8 drops liquid monk fruit sweetener or 1–2 tsp coconut sugar

1 tsp cinnamon

1 tsp ground vanilla bean or 2 tsp alcohol-free vanilla extract

¼ tsp sea salt

4 tbsp dairy-free dark chocolate chips

1 In a food processor, combine ingredients except chocolate chips. Process until completely smooth and the consistency of cookie dough, adding more non-dairy milk if needed. Transfer to a medium bowl and stir in chocolate chips.

2 Enjoy on its own by the spoonful or as a dip with fresh berries or apples. Refrigerate in an airtight container for up to 3 days.

"Happiness for me is largely a matter of digestion."

—LIN YUTANG

CHAI SPICE BLEND

1½ tsp ground cinnamon

1 tsp ground ginger

1 tsp ground cardamom

¼ tsp vanilla powder

¼ tsp ground cloves

¼ tsp ground nutmeg

¼ tsp allspice

GOLDEN MYLK SPICE BLEND

1 tbsp ground turmeric

½ tsp ground ginger

1 tsp ground cinnamon

¼ tsp ground cardamom

pinch freshly ground black
  pepper

AKARSAKA (CUTE)
Chai or Golden Mylk Butter Cups

If you asked me what my favorite candy was growing up, I'd say Reese's peanut butter cups. Today, however, it's these chai or golden mylk butter cups. They're sugar and dairy free, chockful of healthy fats and gut-healing spices, and warming on the digestive system.

MAKES 12

7oz dairy-free dark chocolate chips

2 tsp extra virgin coconut oil

1/8 tsp cinnamon, for dusting

1/8 tsp sea salt, for dusting

FOR THE FILLING

1/4 cup coconut butter

4 drops liquid monk fruit sweetener or
  1 tsp coconut sugar

1 tbsp **Chai** or **Golden Mylk** spice blend

1 Line a mini muffin pan with 12 paper liners. Prepare the spice blend of your choice by stirring spices together in a small bowl.

2 To melt the chocolate, place the chocolate in a glass bowl and set it over a small saucepan of boiling water (or use a double boiler). Add the coconut oil and stir until fully melted and smooth. Remove from the heat.

3 Scoop about 1/2 tbsp melted chocolate into each of the 12 muffin liners, filling them about one-quarter of the way up the side of the liner. Place the pan in the freezer and allow the chocolate to set for 5 minutes. Set aside the bowl with the remaining chocolate.

4 While bottom chocolate layer sets, make the filling. In a small saucepan, melt the coconut butter over low heat until smooth and creamy. Stir in the sweetener and spice blend of your choice. Place in the refrigerator to cool for a few minutes, until the filling is the consistency of peanut butter.

5 Take the muffin pan out of the freezer. To each cup, add 1 tsp spiced coconut butter, pressing it down to flatten. Remelt the remaining chocolate (if needed) and top each cup with 1/2 tbsp melted chocolate.

6 Return to the freezer for another 3 minutes until nearly set. Sprinkle with cinnamon and sea salt, then return to the freezer until ready to eat. These can be kept frozen in an airtight container for up to 1 month.

SANTVANA (COMFORTING)
Coconut Milk Kheer

On the night of *Sharad Purnima,* the full moon harvest festival to celebrate the Goddess Lakshmi and end of the monsoon season, people fast the entire day, drinking only coconut water or milk. Under the moonlight, they prepare kheer, a sweet rice pudding, as an offering to the moon Gods. The kheer sits under the moonlight as rituals are sung, and the sweet dessert is consumed in the morning. Try this sugar- and dairy-free version for your own moon ceremony.

SERVES 6

1 cup brown basmati rice, soaked for 1 hour, rinsed, and drained

4 cups unsweetened vanilla coconut milk

2 tsp cinnamon

1 tsp ground vanilla bean or 2 tsp alcohol-free vanilla extract

1 tsp ground cardamom

12 drops liquid monk fruit sweetener or 3 tbsp coconut sugar, to taste

⅓ cup raisins (omit for Kapha)

TOPPINGS: coconut flakes, chopped pistachios, saffron strands

1 In a large pot or Dutch oven, combine all ingredients. Bring to a boil over high heat, then reduce heat to medium-low. Simmer for about 1 hour, stirring occasionally, until creamy.

2 Serve warm or chilled, garnished with coconut flakes, chopped pistachios, and saffron strands.

Slow cooker: Combine all ingredients and cook on high for 3 hours, stirring once or twice. Take care not to overcook, which will make the milk separate.

You can use quinoa instead of rice, which will reduce cooking time to 15 minutes.

ROPANA (HEALING)
Golden Mylk Truffles

Turmeric may be the most effective nutritional supplement in existence, with countless benefits for your body and brain. Curcumin, the bioactive ingredient in turmeric, can increase neural stem cell growth by as much as 80 percent at certain concentrations. It's best absorbed when paired with healthy fats and black pepper, so these truffles have you covered on all bases.

MAKES 12

⅛ cup coconut oil

½ cup cashew butter (1 cup blended cashews to form paste)

1 tsp ground turmeric

1 tsp cinnamon

½ tsp ground ginger

½ tsp ground cardamom

4–8 drops liquid monk fruit sweetener or 1–2 tbsp coconut sugar

⅛ tsp freshly ground black pepper

½ tsp ashwagandha powder (optional)

½ tsp shatavari powder (optional)

cinnamon, to sprinkle

1 In a large saucepan, warm the coconut oil over low heat until melted. Stir in the cashew butter until completely combined.

2 Add the turmeric, cinnamon, ginger, cardamom, monk fruit sweetener, pepper, ashwagandha, and shatavari, if using. Stir until combined (the consistency should be soft and creamy) and remove from the heat.

3 Pour the mixture into silicone candy molds or paper mini muffin cup liners, using 1–2 tbsp of the candy mixture per piece. Place in the freezer for at least 3 hours or until solid.

To make round truffles, freeze the liquid candy mixture in a container, then scoop out 1 tbsp portions and roll them into balls.

4 Eat straight from the freezer or let sit for a few minutes at room temperature to soften. Sprinkle with cinnamon and enjoy!

NIRVRTI (HAPPINESS)
Chai Bliss Balls

Beat the mid-afternoon slump with these chai-spiced bliss balls. They'll fill you up with plant-based energy as well as extra digestive-boosting, stress-relieving, hormone-balancing benefits.

MAKES 14

- 2–4 tbsp non-dairy milk
- ½ cup coconut oil, melted
- ¼ cup sunflower, almond, or coconut butter
- ¼ cup sunflower seeds
- ¼ cup hemp hearts
- ½ cup raw almonds
- 2 tsp cinnamon
- 1 tsp ground cardamom
- ¼ tsp ground ginger
- ⅛ tsp ground nutmeg
- ½ tsp alcohol-free vanilla extract

- 4 Medjool dates, pitted and preferably soaked
- ¼ tsp sea salt
- 1 tsp ashwagandha powder (optional for adaptogenic benefits)
- ½ tsp shatavari powder (optional for adaptogenic benefits)

Suggested coatings: beetroot powder, hemp seeds, cacao nibs, chopped goji berries, coconut flakes

1 Place all ingredients, beginning with 2 tbsp non-dairy milk, in a food processor. Blend until a wet dough forms. Add another 1–2 tbsp non-dairy milk if the mixture is dry.

2 Divide the dough into 16 2-inch balls and roll in your choice of toppings. Place on a parchment-lined baking sheet and freeze for at least 30 minutes.

3 Before eating, take the balls out of the freezer to thaw for a few minutes. Balls can be stored in an airtight container in the freezer for up to 1 month. They do melt in heat, so it's best to consume them cold.

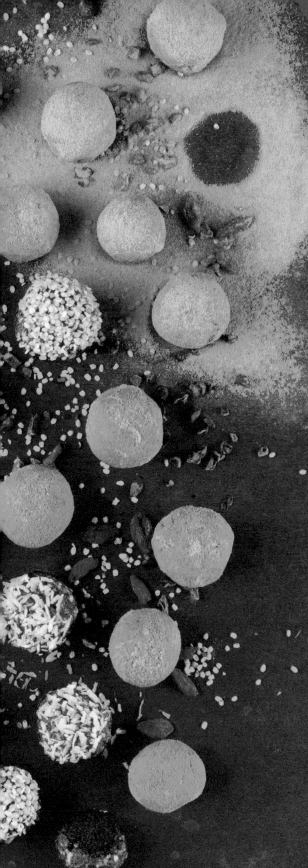

VAIDYA (MEDICINAL)
Golden Mylk Bliss Balls

Ayurveda teaches that we have five-layered bodies, called *koshas* (see pages 76–77). The inner-most layer is our physical body and the outer-most layer is our bliss body. These bliss balls connect both.

MAKES 10

½ cup natural cashew butter

12 drops liquid monk fruit sweetener or 4 pitted dates, preferably soaked

1 tsp turmeric, plus more to coat

½-in piece fresh ginger, grated

½ tsp ground vanilla beans or 1 tsp alcohol-free vanilla extract

1 tsp cinnamon, plus more to coat

⅛ tsp black pepper

⅓ cup blanched almond flour

2 heaping tbsp plant-based protein powder (optional)

⅓ cup pecans, walnuts, or hazelnuts (optional)

1 Place all ingredients except optional nuts in a food processor and process until the mixture is creamy like smooth peanut butter. Add the nuts, if using, and pulse for 10 seconds so they're still a bit rough.

2 Divide the mixture into 10 2-inch balls and roll in turmeric and cinnamon to coat, if desired. Place on a parchment-lined baking sheet and freeze for at least 30 minutes.

3 Before eating, take the balls out of the freezer to thaw for a few minutes. Balls can be stored in an airtight container in the freezer for up to 1 month.

TAVAT (SO GREAT)
Tahini-Date Salted Caramel Slices

Dates are one of those foods that make you wonder how on earth something natural can literally taste like candy. They're full of magnesium and potassium, perfect for after a sweaty yoga session. They're also rich in fiber and can aid weight loss by flushing out toxins and regulating blood sugar levels. However, even natural sugars add up, so be mindful of your slices, especially my Kaphas!

SERVES 16

FOR THE CARAMEL
1 cup pitted Medjool dates, soaked
  1 hour and drained
½ cup tahini
2 tbsp coconut oil
½ tsp cinnamon
½ tsp ground cardamom (optional)
½ tsp ground vanilla bean (optional)
¼ tsp ashwagandha powder (optional)
⅛ tsp sea salt or other finishing salt

FOR THE CHOCOLATE COATING
3 tbsp coconut oil
3 tbsp cacao powder
8–12 drops liquid monk fruit sweetener

1 To make the caramel, combine all ingredients in a food processor or high-powered blender. Blend until a smooth, creamy paste forms, scraping down the sides as needed.

2 Line a 6 × 6in container with parchment paper. Transfer the paste to the container and press it down evenly. Place in freezer while you prepare the chocolate coating.

3 To make the chocolate coating, in a small saucepan over low heat, melt the coconut oil. Stir in the cacao powder and monk fruit sweetener until well combined.

4 Drizzle the cacao mixture over the caramel and sprinkle with salt. Freeze until firm, about 1 hour. Remove from the pan and cut into slices with a sharp knife.

CHITTA (INTENTION)
Chickpea Chocolate Crunch Bark

You may have had chocolate bark with almonds, but probably never with chickpeas. Why chickpeas? Because they're lighter and loaded with protein, fiber, iron, calcium, and essential minerals. They give a nice crunch to the creamy chocolate while revving up its nutritional benefits. Make a double batch to have around for that perfect combination of smooth and crunchy.

SERVES 16

2 cups cooked chickpeas
1 tbsp + 1 tsp melted coconut oil, divided
1 cup dairy-free dark chocolate chips

1 Preheat the oven to 400°F and line a rimmed baking sheet with parchment paper.

2 In a medium bowl, toss the chickpeas with 1 tbsp coconut oil until well coated. Spread the chickpeas in a single layer on the prepared baking sheet and bake for 25 minutes or until crunchy. Let cool on the baking sheet.

3 Line a second baking sheet with parchment paper. Place the chocolate chips and remaining 1 tsp coconut oil in a medium glass bowl and set over a saucepan of boiling water. Stir constantly until the chocolate is fully melted. Remove from heat.

4 Fold the roasted chickpeas into the melted chocolate, stirring gently until fully coated. Spread the chocolate mixture in a thin layer on the prepared baking sheet. Place in the freezer to set for at least 30 minutes.

5 To serve, break the bark into pieces. Store in an airtight container in the freezer.

BALYA (CHILDHOOD)
Cinnamon Date Crispy Rice Bars

Rice crispy treats were my favorite treat growing up, but when I learned how much sugar they have, they became a distant memory... until I created a version made with dates, brown rice, and coconut oil. Sunflower seed butter adds an extra nutty taste, plus protein and iron, and a touch of cinnamon helps to stabilize blood sugar.

SERVES 16

10 Medjool dates, pitted
½ cup sunflower seed or almond butter
2 tbsp non-dairy milk
1 tbsp coconut oil
1 tsp alcohol-free vanilla extract
1 tsp cinnamon
3 cups crispy brown rice cereal
pinch of sea salt

1 Line an 8 × 8in baking pan with parchment paper and set aside. In a food processor, combine the dates, sunflower seed butter, non-dairy milk, coconut oil, vanilla extract, and cinnamon. Blend to form a thick, sticky paste, scraping the bowl as needed.

2 Transfer the date paste to a saucepan and heat over medium heat until soft and warm. (This will make it much easier to mix with the cereal.) Stir in the salt.

3 In a large bowl, combine the rice cereal and date paste and mix until the cereal is evenly coated.

4 Scrape the mixture into the prepared baking pan and spread to the edges, pressing firmly. (Placing an additional piece of parchment paper over the top of the mixture will help to press it tightly into an even layer.) Refrigerate for at least 30 minutes or until firm. To serve, turn out onto a cutting board and cut into 16 squares.

SARASWATI (GODDESS OF CREATIVITY)

Sun-Butter Sweet Potato Brownies

The word "brownie" has become synonymous with "unhealthy" and wrongfully so. Not every brownie needs to have sugar, dairy, flour, eggs, and refined oil. In fact, good ol' sweet potatoes make an excellent base, giving your brownies a fudgy texture and sweet taste as well as making them warming, grounding, and tridoshic.

SERVES 9

2 tbsp ground flaxseed

6 tbsp water

1 large baked sweet potato, skin removed

¼ cup coconut oil, melted

1 cup sunflower seed butter (can sub almond)

4–8 drops liquid monk fruit sweetener (adjust to taste)

½ cup raw cacao powder

1 tsp cinnamon

½ tsp sea salt

½ tsp baking soda

1 cup dairy-free dark chocolate chips

FOR THE SWIRLS

¼ cup sunflower seed butter

1 tbsp coconut oil

4 drops liquid monk fruit sweetener

1 Preheat the oven to 375°F. Grease an 8 × 8in baking dish with coconut oil or line with parchment paper.

2 In a small bowl, make flax eggs by stirring together ground flaxseed and water. Let sit until thickened and gelatinous, about 15 minutes.

3 In a food processor, combine flax eggs and all remaining ingredients, except chocolate chips. Process until smooth, then stir in the chocolate chips. Pour the batter into the prepared pan and spread evenly.

4 To make the swirls, in a small bowl, whisk together the swirl ingredients until smooth. Drop by spoonfuls into the batter and use a chopstick to swirl across the top.

5 Bake for 30–40 minutes. Brownies should be slightly firm on top. Remove from the oven and allow to cool in the pan completely before cutting into squares.

ANANDA (BLISS)
Adaptogenic Fudge

Adaptogens are herbs that help your body deal with stress and promote an overall sense of well-being, called *ojas* in Ayurveda. Ashwagandha means "strength of a stallion" and helps increase energy and handle stress. Shatavari is its feminine form and means "woman with 100 husbands." This lesser-known adaptogen helps balance female hormones, calm the nervous system, and of course, manage 100 husbands.

SERVES 16

1 tsp cacao powder

1 tsp ashwagandha powder

1 tsp shatavari powder (optional)

½ tsp cinnamon

¼ tsp sea salt

¼ cup coconut oil

½ cup sunflower seed butter (can sub almond butter or tahini)

8 drops liquid monk fruit sweetener or 1 tbsp maple syrup

1 In a small bowl, mix together the cacao powder, ashwagandha powder, shatavari powder (if using), cinnamon, and salt.

2 In a small saucepan, gently warm the coconut oil over low heat until melted. Add the sunflower seed butter and monk fruit sweetener and stir until well combined.

3 Once wet ingredients are blended, add the dry ingredients to the saucepan and stir until well combined.

4 Line an 8 × 8in baking pan with parchment paper. Scoop mixture into the prepared pan and place in the freezer until solid, about 1 hour.

5 Once solid, remove from the fudge by lifting the parchment paper out of the pan and cut into 16 pieces. Fudge can be stored in an airtight container in freezer for up to 1 month. It will melt in the heat, so it's best to consume when chilled.

SVATTA (SPICED)
Chai Chocolate Truffles

In supermarkets, you'll see every kind of chocolate: sea salt, mint, orange, marshmallow, even bacon. But for some reason, chai hasn't been represented yet. Let me tell you, chai and chocolate make a great duo. The warming chai spices make the chocolate easier to digest and bring in more of the six tastes of Ayurveda, so you'll actually be satisfied by one truffle (okay, maybe two).

MAKES 12 TRUFFLES

1 cup full-fat coconut milk

1 black tea bag

2 cardamom pods, crushed

1 tsp cinnamon, plus more to coat

½ tsp ground cloves

1 star anise pod

½-in piece fresh ginger, grated

6oz dark chocolate, preferably monk fruit or stevia sweetened

1 tbsp raw cacao powder, to coat

1 In a small saucepan, combine the coconut milk, tea bag, cardamom, cinnamon, cloves, star anise, and ginger. Bring to a boil, then reduce heat and simmer for 5–7 minutes. Strain the liquid into a bowl or large measuring cup and discard the spices and the tea bag.

2 Place the chocolate in a medium glass bowl and set over a saucepan of boiling water. Stir until melted. Add the infused coconut milk to the chocolate and stir until it is well-incorporated, shiny and thick.

3 Remove the bowl from the saucepan and let cool, then refrigerate for at least 2–3 hours.

4 Once the chocolate is firm and mostly solid, scoop out 1-tbsp portions and roll them into round truffles using your hands. If the chocolate feels too soft, return it to the refrigerator until firm.

5 On a plate, mix together the cacao powder and 1 tbsp cinnamon. Roll each truffle in the mixture to coat. Enjoy!

ZOBHA (LIGHT)
Aquafaba Chocolate Mousse

Avocado mousse is great, but if you're looking for the real, fluffy mousse consistency, look no further than aquafaba. Aquafaba is chickpea liquid that makes an excellent egg-white replacer, as it becomes very fluffy when blended, yielding a deliciously light dessert.

SERVES 4

5oz dairy-free dark chocolate, broken into small pieces

1 tbsp almond milk

1 cup aquafaba (liquid drained from 15oz can unsalted chickpeas)

4–8 drops monk fruit sweetener or 1 tbsp maple syrup (optional for extra sweetness)

½ tsp cinnamon (optional)

1 tsp lemon juice or apple cider vinegar (optional for foaming)

TOPPINGS: grated chocolate, pomegranate arils, chopped pistachios

Instead of canned chickpea liquid, you can use cooked chickpeas that have been refrigerated in their cooking liquid for at least 2 days.

1 In a double boiler, melt the chocolate with the almond milk. (You can also place the chocolate and milk in a glass bowl set over a saucepan of boiling water.) Do not stir until the chocolate is completely melted. Once the chocolate has melted into the milk, whisk gently to combine. Transfer the chocolate mixture to a medium bowl to cool.

2 In a large bowl or the bowl of a stand mixer, combine aquafaba, sweetener, cinnamon, and lemon juice, if using. Note: the bowl and any utensils used must be completely free of grease for the aquafaba to whip properly.

3 Using a mixer with a whisk attachment, whip the mixture into stiff peaks. This will take about 8 minutes. Check to see if you have achieved stiff peaks by inverting the bowl. The aquafaba should not slide down at all.

4 If adding sweetener, continue whipping after you reach stiff peaks and add the sweetener drop by drop.

5 Check that the chocolate has cooled (it should not be warm to the touch). Using a silicone spatula, fold about one-third of the whipped aquafaba into the cooled chocolate, then gently fold this mixture back into the whipped aquafaba until fully combined. The mixture may deflate while folding.

6 Pour into 4 small bowls or glasses. Cover and chill in the refrigerator for 3 hours or overnight. Top with grated chocolate, pomegranate, and pistachios.

DHANIKA (RICH)
Avocado Fudge Brownies

Finding an avocado in India is like finding a four-leaf clover.
As incredible as these buttery fruits are, they didn't exist in ancient
India…but that doesn't mean we can't enjoy them! In fact, the oldest
artifacts of avocados date back to 10,000 BCE in Mexico. The
Aztecs called them *ahuácatl*, which translates to "testicle," not only
because their shape but because of their aphrodisiac benefits. So, if
these brownies get you in the mood, don't say I didn't warn ya!

SERVES 9

2 tbsp ground flaxseed

6 tbsp water

2 large or 3 small avocados (more avocado will make fudgier brownies)

½ cup coconut or almond flour

20–30 drops liquid monk fruit sweetener

½ tsp ground vanilla bean or 1 tsp alcohol-free vanilla extract

¼ tsp baking soda

¼ tsp sea salt

4 tbsp cacao powder

FOR THE FROSTING

1 large avocado

8 drops liquid monk fruit sweetener

½ tsp ground vanilla bean or 1 tsp alcohol-free vanilla extract

1 Preheat oven to 350°F. Line an 8 × 8in pan with parchment paper. In a small bowl, make a flax egg by whisking together ground flaxseed and water. Let sit for about 15 minutes until thickened and gelatinous.

2 In a food processor, combine the flax eggs, avocado, almond flour, coconut flour, monk fruit sweetener, vanilla, baking soda, and salt. Process until well combined, scraping the sides as needed, then add the cacao powder and process again until combined.

3 Pour the batter into the prepared pan and bake for 25–30 minutes, depending on how fudgy you would like the brownies to be. If the inside is totally sticky and the brownies don't seem done, don't worry—they will set in the fridge. If you want a cakier texture, bake them for 10 minutes longer.

4 Let the brownies cool completely on the counter, then transfer to the refrigerator or freezer for at least 1 hour to set. (Brownies can be stored in the fridge for up to 3 days before frosting.)

5 When ready to serve, make the frosting. Combine all the frosting ingredients in a food processor or blender and blend until smooth, scraping down the sides to remove any lumps. Spread the avo-frosting over the avo-brownies and enjoy! (Once frosted, brownies should be consumed within 24 hours.)

SUPRIYA (SWEET)
Sweet Potato Pudding

In college, I had a neighbor named Supriya from India. Both of us were really into healthy cooking and instantly became best friends. Since we were on a college budget, almost everything we ate had sweet potato in it—sweet potato salad, sweet potato brownies, sweet potato cereal. This pudding had to be my favorite, though. It requires no blending and is perfect when you want a healthy dessert.

SERVES 2

2 medium sweet potatoes
4 tbsp sunflower seed or almond butter
4 tbsp coconut or almond milk
2 tsp cinnamon

TOPPINGS: full-fat coconut milk, monk fruit or regular maple syrup, hemp seeds, walnuts, cacao nibs, blueberries

1 Preheat oven to 425°F and line a baking sheet with parchment paper. Wash and dry the sweet potatoes and place them on the baking sheet. Bake for 1 hour, until the flesh is tender and easily pierced with a fork. Once cool enough to handle, scoop the flesh from the skins.

2 In a medium bowl, use a fork or potato masher to mash the warm sweet potato flesh with the sunflower seed butter, coconut milk, and cinnamon until thick and creamy.

3 To serve, swirl in a bit of coconut milk and maple syrup and sprinkle hemp seeds, walnuts, cacao nibs, and blueberries over top.

"You are not separate from the whole. You are one with the sun, the earth, the air. You don't have a life. You are life."

—ECKHART TOLLE

Potions

SANTOSANA (COMFORTING)
Golden Mylk

It's safe to say: golden mylk is the new coffee. It revs up the *agni* (digestive fire), reduces inflammation, flushes fat, and increases happiness. In fact, studies have shown that turmeric can be as effective of an antidepressant as Prozac! Drink this every night to stay healthy and happy.

SERVES 1

1 cup non-dairy milk
1–2 tbsp **Turmeric Paste**
2 drops liquid monk fruit sweetener or ½ tbsp coconut sugar
¼ tsp ashwagandha powder (optional)
cinnamon, for topping

1 In a small saucepan, heat milk over low heat until warm. Whisk in turmeric paste, monk fruit sweetener, and ashwagandha (if using).

2 Before serving, froth with an electric frother and dust with cinnamon. Enjoy warm.

TURMERIC PASTE

MAKES 12 TBSP

½ cup water
¼ cup ground turmeric
½-in piece fresh ginger, grated
½ tsp cinnamon
½ tsp ground vanilla bean or ½ tsp alcohol-free vanilla extract
¼ tsp ground cardamom
¼ tsp freshly ground black pepper
¼ cup coconut oil

1 In a small saucepan, combine water and turmeric and bring to a simmer. Add the ginger, cinnamon, vanilla, cardamom, and pepper, and continue to cook, whisking constantly, for 5 minutes.

2 Add the coconut oil and whisk until fully combined. It will have a paste-like consistency.

3 Remove from heat, transfer to a clean airtight container, and refrigerate. Paste can be stored in the refrigerator for up to 5 weeks.

DHAVANA (CLEANSING)
Alkaline Green Juice

Green juice can deliver a ton of nutrients from leafy greens and other vegetables, but most green juices are extremely cooling in nature, which can imbalance our Vata energy. The addition of digestive-enhancing ginger and anti-inflammatory turmeric will rev up your digestive fire so you can absorb even more of your nutrient-dense juice's benefits. Bottoms up!

SERVES 2

4 large handfuls of spinach, rainbow chard, or kale

1-in piece turmeric root or 1 tsp ground turmeric

1-in piece ginger root

1 English cucumber

2 celery stalks

1 lemon, peeled (remove seeds)

handful of parsley or cilantro

pinch of freshly ground black pepper (helps the body absorb turmeric)

¼ cup chopped pineapple (optional)

½ cup raw coconut water (optional)

1 Process all ingredients except coconut water through a juicer.

2 Mix with coconut water, if desired, for additional sweetness.

ANVAHARATI (REPLENISHING)
TURMERIC COCONUT WATER

This is my favorite post-yoga drink. Hydrating coconut water replenishes your body after a sweaty practice, and turmeric enhances muscle recovery, reduces exercise-induced oxidative stress, and even burns belly fat.

SERVES 1

1 cup raw coconut water
1-in piece fresh ginger, peeled
½ tsp turmeric powder
¼ cup lemon juice
pinch of sea salt
pinch of freshly ground black pepper

In a high-speed blender, combine all ingredients and blend until ginger is completely broken down. Strain if desired. Enjoy!

TATKALA (INSTANT)
GOLDEN MYLK CHAI

On the Highest Self Podcast, I joked that I'm not everyone's cup of tea—rather, I'm a cup of golden mylk chai. Hundreds of people wrote in asking for the recipe, so here it is! Try making a big batch of the spice blend for travel.

SERVES 1

1 tsp ground turmeric
½ tsp cinnamon
½ tsp ground ginger
⅛ tsp freshly ground black pepper
¼ tsp ashwagandha powder (optional)
¾ cup hot water
¼ cup non-dairy milk
4 drops liquid monk fruit sweetener or 1 tsp coconut sugar

1 In a mug, mix together the turmeric, cinnamon, ginger, black pepper, and ashwagandha, if using.

2 Add the hot water and stir to combine. Add the non-dairy milk, warmed if desired, and stir well or blend with an electric frother.

3 Stir in monk fruit sweetener and enjoy your official Highest Self Podcast beverage!

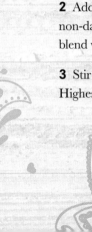

SANTULANA (BALANCING)
DOSHA TEA

Ayurveda is a kitchen science that uses herbs and spices as medicine. Warming spices pacify the Vata Dosha, while cooling herbs balance Pitta. A warming and stimulating blend is best for reducing Kapha.

--- SERVES 1 ---

Vata

½ tsp freshly grated ginger
½ tsp cardamom seeds
½ tsp ground cinnamon or
    1 cinnamon stick
½ tsp ajwain (carom) seeds
sweetener to taste (optional)

Pitta

½ tsp fennel seeds
2 tbsp chopped fresh mint
½ tsp dried rose petals
sweetener to taste (optional)

Kapha

½ tsp freshly grated ginger
½ tsp fennel seeds
¼ tsp cumin seeds
1 whole clove
juice of ½ lemon (add at end)

1 In a small saucepan, combine 2 cups water with the tea ingredients for your Dosha. Bring to a boil, then remove from heat and let steep, covered, for at least 15 minutes.

2 Strain tea through a fine mesh sieve. Enjoy hot throughout the day, taking a sip every 20 minutes for optimal digestion.

"Health, not illness, is our natural state. It's usually just a matter of finding it tucked beneath the layers of imbalance that have accumulated over time."

—DR. SUHAS KSHIRSAGAR

CHANDRIKA (MOONLIGHT)
Chai Latte

For many people, chai lattes are an entry to the world of Ayurvedic spices, but most are full of sugar and don't actually contain real spices. I love making this super sattvic chai concentrate for instant lattes while I work, with the added adaptogenic benefits of ashwagandha and shatavari.

CHAI CONCENTRATE

MAKES 3 CUPS

- 5 cups water
- 12 cardamom pods, crushed
- 8 whole black peppercorns
- 8 whole cloves
- 4 cinnamon sticks or 2 tsp ground cinnamon
- 4-in piece fresh ginger, sliced
- 2 whole star anise pods
- 2 tsp ground vanilla bean or 4 tsp alcohol-free vanilla extract
- ½ tsp ground nutmeg
- 1 tsp allspice
- 4-12 drops liquid monk fruit sweetener or 1-3 tsp coconut sugar
- 5 black tea bags (use rooibos for caffeine-free)

1 In a small saucepan, bring all ingredients except tea bags to boil over high heat. Reduce heat to medium-low, add the tea bags, and simmer for 20 minutes.

2 Remove from heat and strain through a fine mesh sieve to remove solids. Chai concentrate can be refrigerated in a jar for up to 2 weeks.

SERVES 1

- ½ cup non-dairy milk
- ½ cup **Chai Concentrate**
- 1 tsp coconut oil (optional)
- ¼ tsp ashwagandha powder (optional)
- ¼ tsp shatavari powder (optional)
- cinnamon, for topping

1 In a small saucepan, gently heat the milk and chai concentrate until warmed. Stir in the coconut oil, ashwagandha, and shatavari, if using.

2 Pour into cup and froth with an electric frother. Dust with cinnamon and enjoy warm.

POSAKA (NOURISHING)
Spiced Pistachio Mylk

Pistachios don't get the attention they deserve. Not only do they boast a fresh green hue, they're also packed with protein and iron and used as an anemia remedy in Ayurveda. They promote healthy gut bacteria and have been shown to be more effective than almonds at increasing butyrate-producing bacteria in the gut.

SERVES 4

4 cups water

1 cup raw pistachios, soaked 6 hours and drained

½ tsp alcohol-free vanilla extract

⅛ tsp sea salt

½ tsp cinnamon

¼ tsp ground cardamom

¼ tsp ground cloves

¼ tsp fennel seeds

¼ tsp ground ginger

1 Place all ingredients in a high-powered blender and blend until well combined.

2 Place a nut milk bag over a large bowl and pour the mixture into the bag. Tie the top, then lift the bag and squeeze to extract milk into the bowl.

3 Transfer the filtered pistachio milk to a 1-qt jar or pitcher and refrigerate for up to 5 days.

RASAYANA (HEALING ELIXIR)
ASHWAGANDHA COCONUT MILK

Ashwagandha is an Ayurvedic *rasayana*, which are substances that slow the aging process, increase longevity, and increase both physical and mental strength. Ashwagandha particularly increases sexual desire (*vajikara*), rejuvenates the body (*rasayani*), increases strength (*balya*), and clears impurities (*ama*) from channels of the body. Though bitter on its own, it tastes great in this recipe.

SERVES 6

2 cups unsweetened shredded coconut

4 cups filtered water

½ tsp ground vanilla bean

½ tsp cinnamon

¼ tsp ground nutmeg

½ tsp ashwagandha powder

2 drops liquid monk fruit sweetener or your choice sweetener, to taste

pinch of sea salt

1 Place coconut and water in a high-powered blender and blend until well combined. Place a nut milk bag over a medium bowl and pour the mixture into the bag. Tie the top, then lift the bag and squeeze to extract milk into the bowl.

2 Pour into a saucepan, add remaining ingredients, and bring to a near boil. Enjoy warm at night, particularly out of a big mug with two hands and a loving gaze. The way you consume your food and drink is just as important as what they contain.

"Digestion is the subtle process that transforms food into consciousness."

—DR. VASANT LAD

PACAKA
(DIGESTIVE ENHANCING)
TRIDOSHIC CCF TEA

Cumin, coriander, and fennel stimulate the digestive system, help the body remove toxins, and increase nutrient assimilation. CCF tea is recommended to drink throughout the day to keep the *agni,* digestive fire, burning bright.

SERVES 1

½ tsp cumin seeds
½ tsp coriander seeds
½ tsp fennel seeds
4 cups water

1 In a small saucepan, combine seeds and water and bring to boil. Turn off heat, cover, and steep for 15 minutes or even overnight for a stronger brew.

2 Strain into a thermos and sip every 20 minutes throughout the day to keep your digestive system hydrated and your belly happy.

ZARADA (AUTUMN)
GINGER PUMPKIN PIE LATTE

Pumpkins are synonymous with autumn, but did you know they can help sharpen the intellect and induce calm? This is why Ayurveda uses them to treat a variety of mental imbalances, including anxiety and stress.

SERVES 1

1 cup non-dairy milk
2 tbsp pumpkin purée
1 tsp cinnamon
½-in piece fresh ginger, grated
1 tsp pumpkin pie spice
½ tsp alcohol-free vanilla extract
1 tbsp coconut oil (optional)

1 In a small saucepan, combine all ingredients and bring to a simmer over medium heat. Simmer for 5 minutes, whisking occasionally, until heated through.

2 Froth with an electric frother before serving and sprinkle with cinnamon. Enjoy warm.

SHAKTI (DIVINE FEMININE)
Rose Cardamom Latte

Shakti is feminine life force. It's the energy that moves through us, making us feel alive, luminous, and vibrant. While Shiva (masculine energy) observes, Shakti creates. She is the process of intention to formulation to expression. Without her, there would be no life. This rose cardamom latte brings all her divine qualities out to dance.

SERVES 1

1 cup non-dairy milk

4 cardamom pods, lightly crushed

½ tsp rose water

½ tsp alcohol-free vanilla extract

¼ tsp natural beet-derived pink food coloring (optional, for color)

dried rose petals, to garnish

1 In a small saucepan, stir together non-dairy milk, cardamom, rose water, vanilla, and food coloring, if using. Bring to a simmer over medium-low heat for 3–5 minutes.

2 Remove from heat and strain through a fine mesh sieve. Froth using an electric frother, and serve sprinkled with rose petals.

Index

Publisher: Mike Sanders
Editor: Ann Barton
Book designer and art director: William Thomas
Recipe photography: Kelley Schuyler
Travel photography: Aman Chotani
Food styling: Savannah Norris
Recipe testing: Trish Sebben Malone
Proofreading: Laura Caddell
Indexing: Celia McCoy

First American Edition, 2018
Published in the United States by DK Publishing
6081 E. 82nd Street, Indianapolis, Indiana 46250
Copyright © 2021 by Sahara Rose Ketabi

21 22 23 24 25   10 9 8 7 6 5 4 3 2 1
001-310765-DEC2021

ISBN: 978-0-7440-4961-9
Library of Congress Catalog Number: 2018933873

DK books are available at special discounts when purchased in bulk for sales promotions, premiums, fund-raising, or educational use. For details, contact: DK Publishing Special Markets, 345 Hudson Street, New York, New York 10014 or SpecialSales@dk.com.
Printed and bound in China

The publisher would like to thank the following for their kind permission to use their photographs:
Aman Chotani: cover, 6–7, 9(t), 10, 12, 17, 18, 22, 62–63, 80–81, 96–97, 124–125, 152–153, 190–191, 206–207, 230–231, 253
Akshay Chandresh Pandey: 24–25, 38–39
Naman Srivastava: 4, 9(b), 20

All other images © Dorling Kindersley Limited
For further information see: www.dkimages.com

for the curious
www.dk.com

Note: This publication contains the opinions and ideas of its author(s). It is intended to provide helpful and informative material on the subject matter covered. It is sold with the understanding that the author(s) and publisher are not engaged in rendering professional services in the book. If the reader requires personal assistance or advice, a competent professional should be consulted. The author(s) and publisher specifically disclaim any responsibility for any liability, loss, or risk, personal or otherwise, which is incurred as a consequence, directly or indirectly, of the use and application of any of the contents of this book.
Trademarks: All terms mentioned in this book that are known to be or are suspected of being trademarks or service marks have been appropriately capitalized. Alpha Books, DK, and Penguin Random House LLC cannot attest to the accuracy of this information. Use of a term in this book should not be regarded as affecting the validity of any trademark or service mark.

ABOUT THE AUTHOR

Sahara Rose is an ancient soul in a modern body. She has been called "a leading voice for the millennial generation into the new paradigm shift" by Deepak Chopra. She is the best-selling author of *Discover Your Dharma, Ayurveda (Idiot's Guides)*, and *A Yogic Path Oracle Deck + A Yogic Path Journal*. She also hosts the *Highest Self Podcast*, the top-ranked spirituality podcast on iTunes, and is the founder of Rose Gold Goddesses + Dharma Coaching Institute. Discover your Dosha with her free quiz at iamsahararose.com and connect with her @iamsahararose.

ACKNOWLEDGMENTS

Immense gratitude to my husband who came on this trip to India with me, the families who invited me into their homes, the photographers who captured these moments, the editors who brought it to paper, the Earth for providing us with paper, my parents for providing me with life, the universe for providing me with the idea for this book, and you for reading it. All is connected, and I am honored to be a part of the expansion of Ayurveda and consciousness. *Atma Namaste.*